All That It Takes Is
All That You've Got
and
All That You've Got Is
All It Takes

Dion Jordan

PublishAmerica
Baltimore

First printing

ISBN: 1-4137-7174-2
PUBLISHED BY PUBLISHAMERICA, LLLP
www.publishamerica.com
Baltimore

Printed in the United States of America

Dedication

This book is dedicated to my beautiful wife Michele. You are my gift from God. I love and cherish you with all my heart. And to my beautiful daughters Mia and Sydnee for being my inspiration and reason for writing this book.

Solomebin,
may the Lord
smile on you all
and may all your
dreams come true
Dion

Acknowledgments

There are a number of wonderful people who contributed in countless ways to my experiences and knowledge in writing this book.

To my Lord and Savior Jesus Christ who gives me the courage and strength and hope to do all things.

Thank you to my parents Charles and Esther Jordan for all the love and support you have given me over the years.

Thank you to my sister Trish for being my voice when nobody could understand what I was saying.

Thank you to Cobi and Antonio for your faith and encouragment.

Thank you to my Cousin Tony for being the brother I never had and showing me at an early age how to compete and win.

Thank you to my cousin Mike for being the educational pioneer that showed me the difference an education can make.

Thank you to my cousin, Jeff, for teaching me to live every day full of life and laughter and that tomorrow is never promised.

To my Aunty Pat and Uncle Lloyd for all your support and love throughout the years.

Thank you to Grammy for the legacy you have left for my family and me.

To James Amps for being an awesome mentor and role model for me and hundreds of upcoming speakers around the world.

To Sean Carter and Cheryl Ozide for all your hard work in making my dream a reality.

To my Devos brothers and sisters, my Bethel family, and Open Meadow community, I want to thank you for all your love and encouragement.

Table of Contents

Foreword

A few years ago I was speaking at a University in New York and had the opportunity to talk with Dion Jordan. It became apparent that our views and circumstances on the future of our younger generation and adults around the country—converge. Dion's words in this book entertain what I believe and I am more than positive you will become a believer in this young man after you read the first chapter. More important, you will become a believer in yourself!

After reading *All That It Takes Is All That You've Got And All That You've Got Is All It Takes,* I was floored in its down to earth logic and captivating stories. This book takes you on a journey that will enrich and educate the reader. If you only follow a few of his principals, you will double your effectiveness in your life. He is going to be a superstar because he is great at motivating an audience and putting those words he uses on the stage, in writing.

Motivated by his upbringing and his father's great choice of words, Dion takes us on a journey of self-understanding and personal accountability. The powerful anecdotes he uses in getting the reader to understand their value to humanity is simple and yet profound.

All That It Takes Is All That You've Got And All That You've Got Is All It Takes is designed to help you view and experience where you are today so that you may accomplish your wildest dreams tomorrow.

This is a book rooted in spirit and life. His life and blood flows through these pages because this book was not written by a man who studied the subject of overcoming challenges, it was written by a man who is following his dreams. I urge you to read this book and apply his principles. If you do, there is no doubt in my mind that your life will change for the better—and he is hoping the lives of people around you will change for the better. This is a book for you and the people in your community.

I know Dion – you told me years ago that you had a masterpiece – I believe you my brother and so will a lot of other people. I'll always be there for you sir!

    —James Amps III
      President/CEO, AMPS International, LLC

What to Expect from This Book

I wrote this book with several types of people in mind. For the student wrestling with what paths to take in life, for the athlete who desires to push himself or herself to greater heights, for the employees who expected more out of life and themselves, and to all those who dare to dream and who have the courage to try to do what they love for a living.

With so many books out there claiming to have the "simple steps" to success, I have tried to bring a more practical and honest approach. This book was written with a consistent flow of stories, motivation sound instructions, examples and affirmations—all designed to assist the readers to successfully reach whatever goals and desires they have in their life.

One of the greatest accomplishments one can achieve is to achieve one's intended goals in life, the reality of accomplishing that which you put your mind to do. It is for this reason that success is so enthusiastically celebrated and admired—simply because it is so exceptional and difficult to achieve. Yet you have what it takes. Don't wait for someone to give you permission to succeed and achieve. Instead, give yourself permission. Don't wait for someone to give you authorization to do it. Follow you heart, plan your work and work your plan. Stop renting out your life for other peoples dreams. It is time to start owning your own life and living your dreams. You have the power to set yourself free from whatever limitations there may be. You have what it takes to look into the eyes of any obstacles and watch them melt and become your opportunities. It is now time to greet each day with confidence, and an unshakable faith. Your destiny is tapping its foot waiting for you to get up and show up. All that it takes is all that you've got, and all you've got is all it takes!

Introduction

What if everything you could ever want was sitting right in front of you, just waiting for you to grab hold of it? Would you have the courage to reach out and take it? What if you had the power to turn every problem in your life into a stepping-stone that would help you reach your full potential in life? Would you have the valor to use it? What if you had the ability to energize yourself and be motivated for any task that stands in front of you by simply telling yourself, "I can." Would you dare to say it? What if I told you all these things are possible if you first believe in yourself? Would you believe it?

I don't know what it is that you want to accomplish but I do know one thing: if you want it, you can have it. Richard Bach, the author of *Jonathan Livingston Seagull*, once wrote, "You are never given a dream without also being given the power to make it come true." You know this to be true. Somewhere deep within you there is a voice that keeps telling you, I can do this. It is my pleasure, in this book, to empower that voice within you to reach and surpass whatever you put your mind to do.

What is it that has held you back from accomplishing your goal in the past? What do you anticipate being in the way in the future? Though there will be obstacles in your way, I promise there will be more opportunities than obstacles. Oftentimes your obstacles are your opportunities. It is just a matter of recognizing them when they come along. By preparing your mind to turn them into opportunities, you will find those things that used to trip you up will now lift you up!

There is a fable about the way birds first got their wings. The story goes that initially they were made without them. Then God made the wings, set them down before the wingless birds, and said to them,

"Take up these burdens and carry them."

The birds had sweet voices for singing, and lovely feathers that glistened in the sunshine, but they could not soar in the air. When asked to pick up the burdens that lay at their feet, they hesitated at first. Yet soon they obeyed, picked up the wings with their beaks, and set them on their shoulders to carry them.

For some time, the load seemed heavy and difficult to bear but soon, as they continued to carry the burden and to fold the wings over their hearts, the wings grew attached to their little bodies. They quickly discovered how to use them and were able to soar into the air. The weights had become wings. Likewise, with the right attitude and determination you, too, can turn what used to be weights in your life into wings and fly over what used to hold you down.

CHAPTER 1

Believe in Yourself

I was 20 years old and my father was driving me to the airport. During the car ride, we didn't say much. I was busy with my own thoughts. I was headed off to college and quite frankly, I was worried about whether I could make it academically. I was never much of a student in high school. In fact, I finished high school as the 298th student in a class of 303. Was I really "college material?" How could I thrive in college when I just barely survived in high school?

When we pulled up to the curb, I took a deep breath and stepped out of the car. My father handed me my bag and I tried my best to look the part of the confident student. Trying to sound as nonchalant as possible, I said, "Alright, Dad. I guess I'll call you when I make it to my dorm."

My father must have sensed the hesitance in my voice because he replied, "Son, just do your best."

With that, I turned and slowly walked to the entrance of the airport. I was still filled with worry and dread about the challenges to come. I was hoping to hear a word of encouragement; anything to let me know that I would be okay. Just as I made it to the revolving doors, I heard a familiar voice say, "Son, all that it takes is all you've got, and all you've got is all it takes."

At that, I turned to my father and gave him the Jordan nod as if to say, "I got it, Pop." With a spring in my step, I walked through the revolving doors, determined to make a success out of myself.

I have to admit it was not easy, but very challenging. I remember the early struggles of adjusting to the world of college academia. In particular, I vividly recall the frustration of studying really hard for my first exam only to score 9 out of 100. Fortunately, as I walked back to my dorm room, my eyes welled up with tears; I heard my father's words ringing in my ears. Time and time again, whenever I met with frustration, those words came back to me. "Son, all that it takes is all that you got..."

I must confess that there were times when I thought that perhaps my father was mistaken. Perhaps, he had meant to say something like, "All that it takes is more than you got and all that you got ain't a lot," but had somehow mixed the words up. However, in the end, he proved to be correct. It took everything in me to complete college and graduate school, yet everything in me was enough for the task. I found out later that the reason I was able to accomplish this goal was not that my father believed I could, but because I learned how to believe in myself.

To reach your goals in life you have to first believe that you can. In the final analysis, your success in life will not be determined by your education, your background, your contacts, the economy or any other external factor. Your success will be determined by your belief in yourself. As Richard M. DeVos, co-founder of Amway, once said, "The only thing that stands between a man and what he really wants from life is the will to try it and the faith to believe it is possible." I have discovered that there are only two types of people—the people who think they can and they people who think they can't. And the really strange thing is that both types are absolutely correct. The people who think they can achieve their dreams succeed. And the people who don't think they can achieve their dreams don't.

Virgil said it best when he said, "They can because they think they can." It is for this reason that you should start believing in yourself. It is the reason why some people look at problems yet see opportunities, while others look at opportunities but see problems. It has nothing to do with the circumstance itself and everything to do with what they believe.

As a motivational speaker, I know that my belief is the most crucial element to my success on the platform. If I don't believe in the message, then the audience never will. In addition, not only must I believe in the message, but I must believe in the *messenger* as well. For instance, just imagine if you were in an audience and the speaker started his presentation uncertainly by saying: "Well... I have some ideas... well, not really ideas... kind of just thoughts... about how you can improve your lives.... Now, I could be wrong here because after all, who am I? But anyway, since we are all here and we have an hour to kill, let's start...." Would you bother to stay around to hear what the speaker had to say next? I know that I wouldn't. Therefore, if I expect to hold the attention of my audience, I must first believe in my message and in myself.

For some people, believing in oneself comes automatically. They naturally expect the best of themselves. They are expecting to have good things happen to them. They effortlessly exude confidence in themselves and their abilities. They see themselves as a magnet for good things. However, for some people, believing in themselves takes some work. Fortunately, we can all learn to develop the necessary confidence in our own abilities.

So how do you foster your belief in yourself? The first thing that needs to be done is to understand who you really are. Let's take a moment and consider the real you. Not who people say you are or even what you *think* about yourself, but who you are when no one is watching. That's the real you. It's during these moments when you're alone and your actions are no longer determined by what others expect of you, but by what you expect of yourself—that we see the real you. It has been said that the foundation of your success is built in the moments when no one is watching. If your greatest work is done when you know people are watching, they will always fall short of your own expectations, thus it will be harder to build a strong belief in yourself. It's only when you do great things when nobody is around and nobody is keeping track of you that your confidence has a chance to grow. The reason for this is that when you are doing great things because people are watching, chances are you are trying to please them, win their approval, and live up to their standards. Whereas, when nobody is watching and you do great things, you impress yourself, using your own standards and winning your own approval. Remember that being a real success is much better than just trying to look like one. By truly understanding who you really are, you can more easily explore your true beliefs.

The second thing we can do is to explore the different ways in which beliefs are formed by using an everyday example: Let's say you sat in the same chair everyday and the chair never broke. You can say you believe that chair can support you because of experience. So one element of fostering our belief is **EXPERIENCE.**

Now let's say one morning you walk up to this same favorite chair and see that one leg is broken. This is going to cause a change of behavior. Most likely you will not sit in the chair because you see it has a bad leg. Thus we can easily conclude that **WHAT YOU SEE** also dictates your belief.

Now let's say somebody you trust tells you the leg on the chair looks broken but it is still capable of supporting you. Now you may change your behavior and sit in the chair once again. Therefore we can say **WHAT YOU HEAR** plays a role in your belief.

Finally let's say your gut feeling tells you this chair will not hold you. In other words you just know for whatever reason that if you try to sit on that chair you will end up on your backside. As a result, you decide not to sit in that chair. Now we can say **YOUR KNOWLEDGE** plays a role in your belief.

Taking all of these elements under consideration…what have you experienced in your own life that has shaped your positive beliefs in yourself or lack thereof? What victories or failures have you experienced that determine your belief of whether or not you will succeed? In the same way, what do you SEE in yourself when you look in the mirror? Do you see someone you believe in or someone you doubt? What are people saying about you? In other words what do you HEAR? Is it positive or negative? Who and what do you listen to and why do you listen to them? And finally, what do you KNOW about yourself? Regardless of what other people say, think, or do, what do you know to be true about yourself? These are the types of things that we must be protective of when it comes to fostering our beliefs in ourselves.

You should make it a habit to *spend your time around positive influences;* with people who will build you up and support your goals and dreams. Make it a practice to hang around those who will encourage you rather than discourage you. Likewise, you should seek out those smarter than yourself and those who have been where you're trying to go. My teachers used to tell me, if you're the smartest person in your group, you need to find a new group. This may require you to give "pink slips" to those around you that bring you down, or who may be obstacles in reaching your goals. Pink slips are my way of letting someone know their influence or opinions are no longer needed in my life. I keep "pink slips" in my pocket and I would encourage you to do the same. It is important to know who you can count on and who you need to count out! You cannot afford to keep people around whose main goal in life is to bring drama! Sooner or later it will wear you down. Instead, find those that bring you up.

Likewise, you should *keep your eyes fastened to success stories.* Oftentimes, just seeing that someone else has done it can give you the confidence to try it in your own life. This is exactly what happened to the world of track and field when Roger Bannister ran the first mile in under four minutes. Within one month of Bannister's run, 10 other runners had broken the barrier. Within a year, 37 runners had done it. And within two years, 300 runners had broken the four-minute mark.

Amazing, isn't it? In hundreds of years, not one man was able to run a mile in less than four minutes. Yet, as soon as one man did it, hundreds of others were able to follow in his footstep in a matter of months. The simple truth of the matter is that once others saw what was possible for another man to achieve, they then *believed* it was possible for them to achieve the same thing as well.

Something else that is equally important is *to be your own cheerleader.* One of the easiest ways to do this is to think back on your past successes. Whenever you find yourself doubting your abilities in a particular area, just reflect on your past victories.

Reliving your past victories will do wonders for your self-confidence.

Regardless of your current station in life, you are already tremendously accomplished. You've learned many skills and had many accomplishments. When confronted with a new situation, simply relive some of those past victories to boost your confidence.

Perhaps the most challenging area to maintain self-confidence in is the area in which you have already suffered numerous defeats. For instance, let's suppose you want to be a published writer but your last 27 short stories have been rejected. This is where your belief is most severely tested and also where you belief is the most critical. If you don't believe that you can ever accomplish your goal of being a published writer, you will stop writing (or at the very least, you will stop submitting your work for publication). Of course, once you do this, then your lack of belief becomes a self-fulfilling process. Therefore, the key to maintaining your belief in this situation is to remember your past successes—particularly those that didn't come easy to you.

Another way to build your belief in yourself is *to act the part*. In other words, you must start to act like the kind of person you wish to become. If you want to have a more fit physique, then start acting like a fit person. Eat the foods that fit people eat. Exercise like fit people exercise. Many people make the mistake of saying, "OK, when I get in shape, then I will start jogging, playing tennis and eating right." These people confuse cause and effect. You don't eat properly and exercise because you are fit. You are fit because you eat properly and exercise.

One way to act the part is to dress the part. If you want to be a banker, start dressing like one. Similarly, if you want to be an artist, dress like one. Dressing the part will do two important things for you. First, you will start to "feel" like the person you want to be. In return, you will start acting like that person. Second, others will start to treat you like the person you want to become. If you want to test out this theory on your own, then I suggest you visit an upscale department store wearing your best suit (or dress). You will be amazed at how much more deferentially you are treated than if you show up in that same store wearing a pair of ratty jeans and a sweatshirt.

Recently, I had an interesting experience that proves this point. Last summer, I had the good fortune to attend a pastoral leadership conference. Assembled at this conference were some of the country's best known preachers and motivational speakers. For years, I have admired many of these men and women for their talents and gifts. I was very excited about the opportunity to witness these incredible speakers "do their stuff" up close in person. However, at the time, I didn't know just how up close and personal this experience would become.

On the second day of the conference, one of the pastors was giving a talk that was extremely well attended. In fact, it was so well attended that, by the time I arrived at the hall, her speech was sold out. Needless to say, I was disappointed because from the cheering and shouting going on in the hall, this sounded like a presentation that I didn't want to miss.

Well, as luck would have it, one of the ushers came out of the hall and saw me standing around looking pitiful. He asked if I was alone at the conference and I responded that, indeed, I was alone. He said, "Well, there must be at least one empty seat inside, so why don't you come on in." As you can imagine, he didn't have to tell me twice.

However, as we walked up and down the aisles, there didn't seem to be a single empty space in the entire auditorium. Just when I was ready to give up in my search for that all-elusive open seat, the usher said, "I see an empty seat up front." I immediately thought, "This must be my lucky day! Not only do I get the privilege of hearing this incredible speaker but I get to see her from the front of the room." Yet, when I looked towards the front rows, I still didn't see the empty seat.

I explained this to the usher and he said, "Yes, there is an empty seat up there. It's right on the stage." My first thought was that the usher was making a joke but his face showed that he was absolutely serious. I couldn't believe it. Stage seating is usually reserved for the other speakers and other VIPs. For instance, seated on that stage were none other than the Bishop T.D. Jakes and Les Brown, nationally known celebrity motivational speakers.

Of course, the little me immediately screamed, "No! No! No! No! Dion, don't even think about it! I've let you talk me into some crazy schemes in the past but there is no way we are going to get up on that stage with Bishop Jakes and Les Brown." However, it was too late. Before the little me knew what has happening, I was being escorted on stage to sit with the *other* dignitaries.

I will admit that, at first, I felt uncomfortable in such rarified surroundings. However, before long, I began to think that this is where I belonged. In fact, as the speaker continued to hold the crowd spellbound, I began to secretly wish that she would pass me the microphone. After all, I'm a speaker and I had a few things to say to this group as well.

I noticed as I began to think and act the part of a VIP, I began to feel that way as well. And others began to treat me that way. My "fellow" dignitaries began to treat me as one of their own. In fact, as the speaker was making her closing remarks, she acknowledged the speakers on the stage. One by one, she went down the row, shaking hands and lauding the achievements of the assembled VIPs. When she reached me, I stood tall, shook her hand and looked her directly in the eye as if I had been invited to be on the stage and that I was in my "rightful" place. And with that, she treated me accordingly. Of course, not knowing who I was, she couldn't start to expound on all of my wonderful qualities (modesty being, of course, the biggest). So, instead, she simply addressed me as a "man of God" and said, "God bless you!" While on that stage, I began to truly *believe* that I deserved to be there and my actions since that day reflect that belief.

Final Thoughts

One the greatest things about your beliefs are that you control them. Others may influence them, but you are the only one who is in charge of them. With that being said, it may be important to take note of what beliefs you have that hold you back from moving forward. What beliefs do you have that keep you moving ahead? By identifying these beliefs you will be able to take better control of your behavior. People have a way of living their lives according to what they believe. As a result, the best way to change your behavior is to first change what you believe. Take a moment to consider the last time you had a major change of behavior. Most likely, there was a change of belief tied to it. Can you remember what it was? For some people it is a religious belief that caused a change in behavior. For others it was new information or knowledge that led to a change of belief that ultimately led to a changed behavior. Some of our greatest leaders in the world were able to lead by influencing our beliefs, and by doing so they changed our behavior—which led to changes in our world! People like Sir Isaac Newton, Socrates, Jesus, and many more.

Jump-start your goals in life by believing you are the success you want the world to see. When you start looking like success, you begin to start feeling like success, which leads to behaving like success.

CHAPTER 2

If You're Not Living Your Dream, Then Whose Dream Are You Living?

After graduating from high school, I had no particular plans for my future. As a result, I bounced between a few dead-end jobs before reluctantly agreeing to follow my father's advice and footsteps by joining the U.S. Army. Almost immediately, I realized that I had made one of the biggest mistakes of my young life. I got off the plane in Fort Benning, Georgia, to the soothing sounds of a drill sergeant screaming at the top of his lungs claiming to be my "mommy and daddy" for the next six weeks. Before I knew it, I was pushing the ground (The army's way of saying "push-ups"). When I reached the point that I could no longer feel my arms, I was escorted to my barrack where I had the distinct pleasure of meeting 20 other young men who looked worse off than me. They all seemed to have that same scared look, as if they had no idea how they got there. Before long my head was shaved bald, and my mustache was stripped from underneath my nose.

I was miserable! This is not where I wanted to be. How did I let this happen? Never in my wildest dreams did I expect to be in the Army. And while I certainly didn't enjoy my short stint in the Army and would never want to repeat the experience, I have to admit that my ordeal taught me one valuable lesson: if you don't have a plan for your own life, somebody else will.

For many people, they spend so much time and energy doing what they feel is *expected* of them they never do what they truly *want* to do. I can't tell you how many college students I have spoken to who are majoring in fields of study they really don't like. Likewise, I have met hundreds of seasoned adults who have jobs in which they are unsatisfied. How does this happen? Most likely, someone told them it was a good field to go into. For some, they took the only job they felt they could get. For others, the pay was good although they did not love the work. And still for others, it is all they ever knew to do. The list goes on and on. Whatever the reason might be, the bottom line is they are no longer living their dream. Instead, they are living someone else's dream. It's time to stop renting out your life to others and start living the life you always wanted. Imagine waking up each morning excited about going to your job because you love it. A job where your skills and talents had a chance to flourish. Imagine doing what you love and getting paid for it! One of the greatest ways to reach success is to take the path paved with what you love to do. Look at any person who is successful in what they do and you will see a person who loves what they do. Loving what you do has a way of turning things from impossible to possible. When you love what you do there is energy, creativity, and determination simply because of the love that comes with what you do. Confucius said it best when he said, "When you find work that you love, it is not really work at all." Well the same principle rings true when pursuing your dream, reaching your goals, or living out destiny.

For some of us, the hard part is not doing what you love but recognizing what it is you love doing. For those of us who may find it difficult to figure out what some of your passions may be. I have found four simple ways to recognize your passions.

1. What would you do for free?

One of the easiest ways to find out what your passions may be is to take a moment to consider what you would do for free. If you could give yourself a "vacation day" what would you want to spend your time doing? Once you decide what it is you would do for free, you may very well be on your way to finding one of your passions in life.

I once knew a student who would always tell me he had no idea what he wanted to do for a living. According to him all the "good" jobs were reserved for a selected few. One day, I decided to visit him in his dormitory. From the moment I walked in the door I was amazed at all the beautiful photographs hanging on his walls. His dorm was filled with pictures he had taken with his camera. When I asked him why he did not pursue his passion of photography, he simply said there was no money in it. However, that could not be further from the truth. A wise man once told me, "Do what you love and the money will follow." If you really love what you are doing, chances are that sooner or later you're going to be good at it. As a result, you could be amazed how much money you could make actually doing what you love to do. I have met people all around the world doing things that I never knew you could get paid for doing. I have met women who are professional shoppers. They actually get paid to go shopping! I have met young men who get paid to play video games. They are video game testers.

There is always someone who is willing to pay you for that which you would otherwise do for free.

When I first had an interest in being a motivational speaker I spoke to schools, churches and to anyone who was willing to listen. I was not a bit concerned about getting paid because it is what I loved doing. As time went by, I got better and better at motivating people and keeping their attention. Before long, organizations began to pay me for my services. I will admit, starting out if I made $25 dollars I thought I was doing well. Nowadays, I make thousands! Simply by doing what I love—and the best part about it is that I would do it for free!

2. Check your inventory!

A second way to discover some of your passions in life is to consider what you already have. You would be amazed how many people overlook this one simple thought when it comes to finding their passion. Most people never consider their skills, gifts, interest or talents as a way of making a living. We have an abundance of skills to accomplish anything we may ever decide to pursue in life. There is no need to look any further for opportunities; many times we carry the opportunity we are seeking. In the introduction to this book, I introduced the concept that you already possess everything you need in order to have everything you want. For some people, this is a very difficult concept to grasp. After all, if we already possess everything we need to have what we want, why don't we have it? The answer is that many people don't know what they possess.

I am reminded of the soldiers who returned home after the Revolutionary War. These soldiers returned home to rebuild their lives with varying degrees of success. One particular soldier, while valiant in battle, had a difficult time finding his place after the peace. For many years, this soldier wandered from town to town living from hand to mouth. One day, the poverty-stricken soldier, by then an old man, found himself in a settlement on the western frontier asking for handouts from the settlers there. One of the settlers noticed a small pouch hanging from the old man's neck and asked about its contents. The old man explained that he had received the pouch years ago as a present but had never examined its contents. Curiosity must have finally gotten the best of the old man. He opened the pouch and removed a crumpled, stained note. The note was the soldier's discharge issued by the federal army. This discharge was signed personally by General George Washington and entitled the man to a lifetime pension. Sadly, this man had spent his life in poverty when he possessed a lifetime pension.

This often happens because they don't take an accurate count of their personal inventory. Let's face it. All the money in the world won't buy you a stick of bubble gum if you don't know that you possess it. Likewise, all of the skills and talents in the world won't bring you any closer to your dreams unless you know what those skills and talents are. Therefore, the first step to getting what you want out of life is to start by examining what you already have. Once you do, I believe that you will discover that what you have is *more than* enough.

The problem that many people have in this regard is that they start from the standpoint of what they lack. "I don't have a college degree, so I can never reach upper management." "I don't have the right connections, so I can never succeed in business." "I don't have the 'gift of gab,' so I can never succeed in sales." However, this approach completely ignores all of the talents, skills and abilities that the person does possess. The simple truth is that *each* person on this planet is born with a treasure trove of riches.

Sadly, we are often blinded from this truth because we can only see what we don't have rather than what we have. The truth of the matter is that it is not what you don't have that holds people back, but what they think they need. Therefore, I want us to take a moment to get clear about our capabilities as opposed to our liabilities. You will never run out of room to grow and expand. Your capabilities are immeasurable. You will never run out of new ideas, there will always be new paths to follow. You have skills and talents that have been untouched. Did you know that each person has approximately 700 different skills in their repertoire? 700! It is now time to tap into all these skills and put yourself where you belong—on top.

3. What do you dislike?

Most people think about what they love when considering their passions. This is probably the simplest way to consider what their passion may be. However, considering your dislikes can be just as effective in finding your passion. For example most people who work for organizations such as MADD (Mothers against drunk drivers) do it not because of their love for drunk drivers but because of their strong negative emotions towards drunk drivers. As a result, they get up each morning with a strong passion to bring an end to what they strongly dislike. In return, they live a very satisfying life, knowing they are making a positive difference in the lives of others.

Once again, when we speak about what we love and what we dislike, we are speaking to the emotions that are tied with it.

Emotions are what often give purpose to that which we do. There is something about having strong emotions tied to what you do that motivates people. Your emotions can be the inspiring force that puts your entire being in a state where it can march forth and reach your desire. The stronger the emotion that is tied to the desire, the more determined you will be. Think about the last time you were passionate about something. Can you recall the feelings and emotions that came with your passion?

If, by chance, it is difficult for you to get excited about that which you dislike, remember you can always "flip" your dislike over and find what you love. Using the same example as above, for every mother who dislikes drunk drivers there is a love for safe communities and families. Likewise, for every person who dislikes discrimination there is a love for equality. In the end finding what you dislike is just another route to find what you love.

4. Choose your "Big Ticket."

For some people it's not hard finding what their passions are, but figuring out which passions to pursue first. There are many different theories about how to narrow down your choices. Some people suggest that you write a comprehensive list of everything you'd ever want to see, do or be in life. Others suggest that, instead, you write out your obituary in advance, highlighting all of the achievements you will accomplish throughout your life. And while each of these methods is acceptable, they can be rather daunting. After all, a typical grocery list will have 20 items on it. A lifetime grocery list could contain hundreds (if not thousands of items). Likewise, writing your obituary requires you to plot out your entire life in advance. For many people, it's hard enough to know what they will be doing next Tuesday.

Therefore, you may find it easier (and more effective) to simply write out the "big ticket" items on your lifetime grocery list. In other words, you may just want to write out your biggest or most important goals. In doing so, you may want to confine your original list to just three or four items. By doing this, you won't get lost trying to do too much and never accomplishing anything. Hopefully, by narrowing your goals to the "Big Ticket" items, you will save yourself from becoming a Jack of all trades and a master of none.

Final Thoughts

One of the greatest things you can ever do is to achieve what you have always yearned to do. There is no better feeling than to set your sights on a target and hit it. And this is why success is so celebrated and admired, because it's rare. Very few people will ever invest the time and effort in themselves necessary to reach their goals. However, you're different. You were willing to invest the time and effort to read this book, so I know you have what it takes and all it takes is all you've got.

So give yourself permission to achieve your wildest dreams. Don't wait for anything or anyone to give you permission, renting out your life for other people's dreams. And certainly, don't wait for the "perfect" time or your big break. Follow your heart, use your head and take it upon yourself to make it happen. Plan your work and work your plan. It's time to start owning your life and living your dreams. It's time to greet each day with confidence and an unshakable faith. Your destiny is in your hands.

There are some things that you do better than almost anyone. It is my belief that we have all been endowed with a distinct set of skills and talents and that there is some unique contribution for each of us to make. Regardless of what your talents and skills may be, you can change the world if you so choose. Consider the powerful example of the power of ordinary actions: the success of the civil rights movement in the 1960s. In just a few years, these brave men and women accomplished more for racial equality than had been accomplished in the 200 years before. However, as you will remember, they didn't produce these outstanding results by using great feats of strength or skill. Instead, the civil rights movement consisted largely of two simple actions—sitting and walking. The participants in this movement staged sit-ins at lunch counters and they marched through the streets. Think about it for a moment.

Perhaps the greatest attitudinal shift in the history of this nation resulted from these simple actions.

The bottom line is, you are going to spend most of your time in this life doing something, and so why not spend it doing something you love to do. Whatever you can imagine doing, there is somebody that is going to get paid to do it. So why not let that somebody be you!

CHAPTER 3

Silencing Your Inner Critic

On the opening night of an opera, famous tenor Enrico Caruso was waiting in the wings, preparing to make his appearance before a packed house. Suddenly, the tenor began to shout, "Get out of my way! Get out! Get out!" The stagehands were all shocked because no one seemed to be near him. Nevertheless, at the appropriate time, Caruso took the stage and proceeded to give his usual stellar performance. After the show, one of the stagehands approached Caruso and asked about the commotion backstage. Caruso simply explained, "I felt within the big me that wants to sing and knows it can, but it was being stifled by the little me that gets afraid and says I can't. I was simply ordering the little me out of my body."

Have you ever experienced this type of internal turmoil in your own life? The big you wants to audition for the play at the local community playhouse but the little you says, "Oh, please! You haven't acted since high school." Or the big you wants to go back to school to finish your degree but the little you says, "Get real! You know you're a slow learner." Or the big you wants to ask your dream girl/guy for a date but the little you says, "Are you nuts? Don't you remember how embarrassing it was when that person from the flower shop turned you down? Do you really want to go through that humiliation again?"

It seems that the moment we decided to do something great, step out of our comfort zone or move towards our dreams, a little voice on the inside says, "It won't work. You will never make it. Don't embarrass yourself." I truly believe that inside each of us there is a battle raging. This battle is between the person we are afraid people will see (the little me) and the person we were meant to be (the big me). The little you is concerned about what your friends and family will say about you. The little you worries mainly about what others think. It attempts to keep you from doing anything that may cause you to look unfavorable in the eyes of others.

However, the big you knows your true potential. It knows that you have the ability inside of you to accomplish anything you desire. It wants you to break free of your self-imposed limitations and start living the life you were meant to live. Therefore, it is constantly in battle with the little you.

Now, lets take a moment to imagine how it would be to go through life without ever listening to the "little you." Think of all the concerns that would vanish. No longer would you hesitate to do what needs to be done. No longer would you bite your tongue and not say what needs to be said. You'd be free to speak and act without the worry of what others think. You would have courage beyond measure because you'd be completely immune to the fear of rejection and what people thought of you. Hurt feelings, worry and embarrassment would be eliminated. Imagine how much you could get done, not to mention the clear and refreshing sense of freedom it would bring. You would be free of many of your own limitations.

The "Little Me" Is The Enemy!

There is an African Proverb that states: "If there's no enemy within, the enemy without can do us no harm." The enemy inside is our "little me." The "little me" in most of us is concerned about what others think. It perceives that it is protecting you from embarrassment in the eyes of others. However, what others think of you is irrelevant. The best-selling author and speaker Terry Cole Whitaker's, *What You Think of Me is None of My Business* is one of my favorite books. I believe this is the idea we should all take with our little selves. When he or she starts with questions about what other people will think of you, you can simply say, "What they think of me is none of my business!"

This is particularly true because other people are not really thinking about you, anyway. Most people are concerned about their own "embarrassments" and they do not have much time to give a second thought whether you are making a fool of yourself. As Ethel Barrett once said, "We would worry less about what others think of us if we realized how seldom they do."

I think we have all learned this the hard way at some point or another. For instance, there have been times when my wife, Michele, whom I affectionately call Wifey, has come home with a new hairdo or a new dress and I've been oblivious. On those occasions, I tell her that she is so naturally beautiful that I did not notice the subtle change. Although Wifey is a statuesque beautiful lady, this is not the whole truth. Part of the truth is, *on occasion*, I was so preoccupied with other things that I failed to see the subtle change. We have all experienced the disappointment of achieving a milestone that was important to us but did not mean much in the eyes of our loved ones. Perhaps, you finally lost that ten pounds or received a promotion at work or alphabetized your CD collection. Surely, if your triumphs can fail to register with those closest to you, just imagine how much impact they have on distant relatives, work colleagues and complete strangers. Not much, right?

The same thing is true of your setbacks. The little you sometimes holds you back by pointing out what others will think if you fail. However, the truth is these other people probably couldn't care less one way or another. For instance, in my journey to become a professional speaker, I went through a learning process. I was not always the engaging, witty (not to mention modest) speaker that I am today. However, I can guarantee that there is not a single person anywhere in America who is thinking right now about one of my less than stellar performances. No one is saying, "Hey, I wonder where that Dion guy is. I hope he quit the speaking business."

The same thing applies to your not-so-winning moments. Perhaps you were assigned to give a presentation at work and your presentation fell flat. Trust me, there is no one on your job who stays awake at night and saying, "Oh man, Sally really messed that one up!" The same is true if you submitted your poetry in a contest and did not win the first prize (or even honorable mention). None of the judges is losing sleep over your lackluster sonnet. The only person who cares at all is the little you. And guess what? What he or she thinks about you is irrelevant. Let us assume that I am wrong and there is someone in the universe who is assigned the task of keeping track of your failures. Even if this is the case, you must ignore your critics. Heeding the words of your critics will keep you from ever becoming the big you.

Keep Your Past Behind You

The second way in which the little you attempts to hold you back is by using your past against you. Let's face it. We have all had our share of embarrassing moments. We have all made our share of mistakes. In fact, there is a word for people like us—we are called "human beings." The big you understands that you have made some mistakes. In fact, as we will discuss later, these mistakes are an invaluable part of your future success.

However, the little you sees your past mistakes as evidence of who you are. Of course, nothing could be further from the truth. To quote Anthony Robbins, "Your past is not your future." In fact, your past is not even a reliable indicator of your future. If this were the case, then how would you explain someone like Harry S. Truman? In 1922, Truman's men's clothing store went bankrupt. Yet, 23 years later, he was the president of the most powerful nation on the globe. His past failure as a business person did not indicate his future success as a politician. The truth of the matter is his past had nothing to do with his future success, and neither does your past.

Your worth is not determined by what you have done. Remember, you are not a human *doing*, you are a human being. Your worth is predicated on who you are and who you are, has very little to do with your past setbacks. I once saw this illustrated by a great speaker. He stood in front of the audience and held up a $100 bill. He then asked if anyone in the audience would like to have the $100 bill. As you can imagine, almost everyone did (including me).

He then proceeded to crumple the dollar in his hand. He asked if we still wanted the bill. And, of course, we did. He then dropped the bill and, using his heel, ground it into the floor. Once again, he asked if we still wanted the $100 bill and, of course, we did. Short of setting fire to the bill, there was nothing he could have done to deter our interest in having that bill. And the reason was simple—because even crumbled, smashed and mangled, that bill was every bit as valuable as a crisp, new $100 bill. Remember, your value remains the same although you may have been crumbled, smashed and mangled you are still as valuable as you ever were. The big you has not been damaged by your past. It is waiting for its opportunity to be unleashed and the only thing holding it back is the little you.

Though the past cannot be changed, still it is valuable for what it can teach. The beauty of our past is that we can take from it only that which is useful, and transcend the rest. Your past does not control you. You control it. It influences you in whatever way you allow it to do so. Take the best from the past, and use it to build your own bright future.

For an example, I was born with bowed legs and my feet facing one another. I had a severe case of what is known as pigeon toe. By the age of 8 months, my mom and dad followed the physician's advice and had my legs restrained in braces in hopes that this would correct the problem. I wore these braces every night until I was 2 years old, but to no avail. I would try my best to walk straight and have my feet pointing ahead of me instead inward but I could not do it. Later, I credit my older sister Trish, for coming up with what I thought was a solution. She said, "Put your shoes on the wrong feet which might make your feet look straight. I tried, but all that did was to make my feet hurt.

I was always one of the very last children picked when teams were chosen for sports. The one time I was chosen first, I was chosen for the wrong reasons. I can remember one particular day I was chosen first to be on a kick ball team. I didn't understand why I was chosen first but it felt good to be finally wanted instead of having teams fighting over which team *had* to take me.

As the first kid chosen, I had the distinct honor of being allowed to have my turn to kick the ball first. The ball was rolled to me and I gave it a mighty kick. Unfortunately, because my right foot pointed left, that's exactly where the ball went—left. As the ball traveled severely out of bounds, the kids erupted in laughter. In fact, some of the kids even took to rolling around on the ground and laughing. This cackling band of hyenas included my own teammates and the boy who chose me to be on his team. At that point, I realized that I had been chosen to be the butt of their jokes that day.

Unfortunately, my legs were not the only things crooked. My tongue had problems as well. I stuttered when I spoke and I often slurred my words. I also had trouble with enunciation. For this reason I spent my recess hours with a speech therapist learning how to speak clearly. To others, who might have seen me as a child walking and heard me talking, I may have looked crumpled, but to Trish, mom and dad, I still had as much worth as the crushed $100 bill in the above story. I did not enjoy any of the things I had to go through to correct these childhood problems, but if I had known then what I know now about my future, I would have never complained. Thirty years later I am standing tall and earning a living speaking professionally. I am so glad that my past did not equal my future!

Final Thoughts

Everything that happens to you or around you results in you having an inner conversation with yourself. Your brain is always processing something and sending you a message (or conversation). For example, as soon as you hear the phone ring you may ask yourself, "Who is calling me?" or perhaps, "I wish people would stop bugging me." When something bad happens to you your inner conversation may be "why me" or "this is terrible." Even something as innocent as a stranger saying "Hello," will result in you having an inner conversation. Whether your inner conversation is "do I know this person?" or "They were friendly," I promise you there is some inner conversation going on.

The key here is to be aware of your inner conversations and foster them to work for you and not against you. It has been said that life is 10% what happens to you and 90% how you react to it. I am convinced that your inner conversations plays a big part in how you will react. You can *choose* to have a negative inner conversation or a positive one. Let's say you went to a job interview for your dream job and they said you were not the candidate chosen. What is your inner conversation going to be? Are you going to talk down to yourself and say " I was not good enough" or are you going to tell yourself "Next time, I will make sure they know I am the best candidate." When the man or woman you have a crush on tells you they are not interested in you, what will inner conversation be? Will your conversation be "I am not good enough or pretty enough," or will your inner conversation be "Their loss!"?

Nothing can discourage you as long as you have the right inner conversation going on with yourself. Make it your practice from this day forward that no matter what happens you will carry an inner conversation that will keep you moving towards your goals and not running from them.

CHAPTER 4

Getting Started

You Are Here

On the day after Thanksgiving, I set out for the Lloyd Center Mall here in Portland, Oregon. I was in search of a locket as a gift for Wifey as my way of saying, "Thank You" for allowing me to take the time to write this book. Things were looking good because I had a goal—the locket. Not only that, but I even had a specific destination in mind—the Things Remembered store. In fact, to make sure that I remembered the name of the store, I had written it down on a piece of paper. And get this... I actually remembered to bring the piece of paper with me that day. What could go wrong? Everything.

For one, the Lloyd Center Mall is one of the largest malls in Oregon. Furthermore, as you know, the day after Thanksgiving is one of the busiest shopping days of the year. As a result, the mall was a madhouse to say the least. To complicate matters, although I knew where I wanted to go, I had no real idea how to get there. As a result, I started to get distracted by the various attractions at the mall that day.

I became engaged in conversations about switching my cell phone plan. I became mesmerized by the Santa with the soggy lap. I then found myself wandering into various stores and buying things that I hadn't set out to purchase in the first place. Now, I was starting to feel the pressure because the mall was closing in thirty minutes and I was no closer to getting Wifey her gift (although I had picked out a few nice gifts for myself).

Getting more and more desperate by the minute, I decided to swallow my pride and ask my fellow shoppers for directions. In total, I asked three different people for directions to Things Remembered. And in total, I received three different answers in three different directions for how to get there. I started to really panic when I ran into the solution… literally. In my confusion, I walked right into the mall directory sign.

After looking around to make sure that no one was laughing at me, I thought, "How wonderful! This is just what I needed!" The mall directory had all the information I needed to finally reach my destination. It had a listing of all the stores in the mall. I was pleased to learn that Things Remembered was one of the stores in the mall. Also, the directory contained a map of the entire mall and sure enough, lodged between Zales Jewelers and The Hat Store was Things Remembered.

While I was certainly pleased to know the location of my destination, I was still no more equipped to find it because I didn't know where I was in relation to the store. Did I need to turn left or right? Did I need to go upstairs or downstairs? Fortunately, the people who make these directories are very smart people and they include a very important piece of information on the directory just for this purpose. That piece of information is a big red dot with a caption that reads: "YOU ARE HERE." Armed with this last piece of information, I was able to reach the store and purchase the locket in just 15 minutes.

While my mall adventures were somewhat comical, it's analogous to the situation that many of us encounter when we attempt to reach our goals in life. First of all, I'd like to point out that my only saving grace on that day was that I actually had a specific goal in mind. Can you imagine the mess I would have found myself in had I gone to the mall to get Wifey "something nice?" I'd probably still be there now switching cell phone plans and trying on Air Jordan shoes at the Foot Locker. As a result, the first step to getting started is to get a clear picture of your present. Where are you? After all, to get from here to there you must know where "here" is as well as where "there" is.

However, even a clearly defined goal isn't always enough. You must have a plan or a strategy to accomplish your goal. Obviously, I didn't have such a plan and as a result, I allowed distractions to pull me off course. The same thing happens in life when we have a goal but no real idea of how to reach it. For instance, let's say that your goal is to be a film maker so you sell all of your belongings and move to Hollywood. Unless you have a precise (and effective) strategy for becoming a film maker, you're likely to get distracted by the need to earn a living, fight the daily traffic and going to all of the "hot spots" in town. As a result, you will likely find yourself getting no closer to your ultimate destination.

Also, without a plan or strategy, many people begin to do what I did, they desperately seek advice from anyone. Of course, this is almost never effective. It's not that other people don't want to give you good advice, it's just that they often don't know the answers themselves. That's why the old adage is true: "The fool asks the wise man for advice, while the wise man asks the experienced."

However, many of us become so desperate for advice that we seek it out from anyone willing to give it. And sadly, just about anyone is willing to give it. For instance, when I was wandering through the mall asking strangers for directions, everyone had a solution for me. No one said, "You know, I just don't now." Instead, people gave me bad directions with authority and conviction. I don't think that people were purposefully trying to mislead me. They simply didn't know where the store was located. And even worse, they didn't know that they didn't know.

Yet, to me, all of the advice seemed sound. Why? Because I was equally clueless. It was the classic example of the blind leading the blind. Sadly, this is just what happens to people when they ask for advice from people who haven't "been there." They get lots of advice and much of it seems reasonable. Yet, the only way to know that you are getting good advice is to receive it from someone who knows the way because they've been there already themselves.

Another danger of not having a game plan is that people may talk you into "buying in" to their dreams for you. This is what happened to me in the mall as I began to wander into various stores. My original goal was to buy a locket for Wifey. However, I ended up buying things other than a locket as I met salespeople who had their own agendas. Of course, it was only right that they tried to sell me their products because let's face it, that was their job. Their employers didn't pay them a salary to keep me on course in reaching my goal. They were being paid to pursue their employer's agenda—to sell the products in that store.

Well, in our journeys to success, we will often meet people with their own agendas. If we don't have a clearly defined path to our goals, we may end up being sidetracked. This happens all too often in life. For example, many young adults have aspirations for careers as radio or television announcers. As a result, they get entry-level positions at a radio or television station. Sadly, for many of them, this is as far as they've thought it out.

Before long, the manager of the station has a need for someone in, say, the advertising department. The manager decides to meet his need by asking the eager young intern if he or she would like a higher-paying job in advertising. Because the intern has no set plan for getting from his or her current position to behind the microphone or behind the camera, he or she accepts. Sadly, while this move meets the manager's objective of securing advertising for the station, it doesn't do much for the young person's dream of being an on-air personality.

Finally, establish a deadline for achieving your goal. Without a deadline, you won't have any real impetus to get going or to change strategies when things aren't working. Back to the mall story, I didn't really begin to get serious about Wifey's gift until I realized that the mall was going to close in 30 minutes. I probably would have been content to waste several more hours wandering aimlessly. Fortunately, that wasn't an option. I knew that they weren't going to keep the mall open just for me so that I could make my way to Things

Remembered when I got around to it. Therefore, I became motivated to find the store *quickly*.

Most of us work backwards in reaching our goals. In other words, we know what we want and when we want it and then we make our plans accordingly. For instance, let's suppose you decide to meet some friends for dinner at 7 p.m. on Saturday at a certain restaurant 15 miles from your home. Given this information, you then make your plans for getting ready for the evening. You figure it will take you 30 minutes to drive to the restaurant so you plan to leave your home at 6:30. You then figure it will take you 45 minutes to get showered and dressed for the evening, so you plan to start your preparations at 5:45. However, just imagine how chaotic it would be if you decided to get together "some time" on Saturday evening. What time would you start to get ready for the evening? What time would you leave your house? Who knows, right? This is why it's so important to establish a deadline in your Master Plan.

For all of these reasons, it's critically important to develop a good plan to reach your intended goals. And the first step in developing your plan is to determine where you are now. Where you are now becomes the starting point to take you to where you want to go. Just as in my mall adventure, without this little piece of information, you have little chance of reaching your goal.

We have discussed the importance of getting clear on your goals. However, I now have a confession to make. None of these things will work unless you work. Without the will to get started, all of your dreams are once again just that—*dreams*.

In most cases, the key distinction between those who achieve their goals and those who don't is that the achievers use their backbones while non-achievers rely solely on their wishbones. A dream will only take you so far. You have to travel the rest of the way under your own power. Or as Ben Stein once said, "Nothing happens by itself; it all will come your way, once you understand that you have to make it come your way, by your own exertions."

Of course, I think that most people realize this truth but they nonetheless get stuck on the launching pad of life because, truth be told, starting is the hardest part. In fact, in many cases, getting off the launching pad takes more effort than the rest of the trip. For instance, when the Space Shuttle takes off, it expends more fuel in the first few miles of flight than it expends over the rest of its journey. As it tries to break the hold of gravity, the Space Shuttle fires its thrusters at full blast. In fact, during its first few seconds of flight, it seems to be just inching forward. However, before long, the craft is hurtling through the sky at tremendous speeds. At this point, it releases two large fuel tanks because at that point, they are no longer necessary. The hard part of the trip is over.

Well, the same thing happens to us in life when we embark on a new destination. At the beginning of the journey, we have to push against that great force of nature— inertia. For instance, if your goal is to lose weight, your hardest challenge will be in denying yourself that first slice of cheesecake. In fact, the first day on a diet is by far the most difficult day. The same thing applies to quitting smoking or any other destructive habit.

This same principle applies to not only "give up" goals but also "go up" goals. For instance, any salesperson will tell you that the hardest sale to make to a client is the first sale. To make that first sale, a salesperson may have to call, visit, cajole or downright beg the client for her business. However, the second sale is always much easier. And the 100th sale seems to just happen automatically. The same is true for starting your first business, writing your first screenplay or whatever else you want to accomplish in life. The first time is always the hardest.

Sadly, this fact of life prevents many people from ever getting out of the starting blocks in the race of life. They put off getting started until "the time is right." However, the truth of the matter is that there is no "right" time to get started. There will always be some reason as to why they should wait—the kids are still in school, the kids are out of school, the weather is too cold, the weather is too hot, the economy is too bad, the economy is too good, and the list goes on and on.

If you and I are ever going to turn our dreams into realities, then we have to get started, even when the time is "wrong." After all, just getting started is 90% of the battle. That being said, we are all guilty of procrastinating from time to time. However, I have learned three key ways of turning procrastination into determination.

The first is to *focus on the benefits*. Often, we put off doing what we should do because we put too much of our focus on the burden and not enough focus on the benefits. For instance, let's suppose that you've been putting off sending out a mailing for your business. You simply aren't looking forward to creating all of the mailing labels, writing the letters, making the copies, stuffing the envelopes and lugging all the pieces to the post office. And as long as you continue to focus on the burdens of doing the mailing, you'll find it difficult to actually get the mailing out.

However, instead, try putting your focus on the benefits to be obtained from doing the mailing. Think about the extra sales or donations you will receive as a result of this mailing. When you focus your attention on the benefits, it becomes easier to approach the task. In fact, you begin to look forward to it.

In a sense, this is the secret behind all great achievements. People who are able to demonstrate great courage in the face of persecution, attack and even death are those who focus on the benefits. The brave men and women of the civil rights movement surely could not have enjoyed being beaten and arrested. What would make them get up bright and early to endure the pain? They were focused on the benefits of racial equality for themselves and perhaps more importantly, their children.

The second key for overcoming procrastination is to *change your attitude about the task in front of you*. Above we discussed one way to change your attitude—by focusing on the benefits. Another way to change your attitude is to change your vocabulary. Often, when we describe our tasks for the day, we describe them as things we "have to" do. This is the wrong way to look at it. They aren't things we have to do; they are things we *get* to do.

For instance, if you have decided to lose weight by jogging a mile each morning before work, don't get out of bed and mumble about *having* to run a mile. After all, the truth of the matter is that you don't *have* to do anything. You are *choosing* to take some action to increase your long-term health and your current energy levels. And you're lucky to be able to do so. There are many people who aren't as fortunate as you are; they don't have use of their legs. These people would give anything to be able to do what you think you *have* to do.

Likewise, many people get up each morning grumbling about having to go to work. However, they don't have to go to work; they *get* to go to work. There are millions of people in our country who are unemployed. These people would love the opportunity to support their families through gainful employment. These people would love to be able to contribute to society and enjoy the respect that comes from doing a job and doing it well.

As you can see, it's all really a matter of attitude. When you change your attitude about what you *have* to do, you soon realize that it's not a burden, it's a privilege.

The simple truth of the matter is that there is no way to avoid the fact that you're going to have to expend some effort to get what you want out of life. I'm reminded of this fact when I drive down the streets of downtown Portland and see people panhandling for money. Some look upon these people and dismiss them as lazy. However, let me assure you that even for them there is no way around effort. I've come to see them as anything but lazy. I know that I couldn't stand outside all day in weather as cold as 10 degrees and as hot as 100 degrees. Nor could I handle all of the rejection and snide remarks that people make. The simple truth of the matter is that it's harder for them to do what they do than for me to do what I do for a living.

The bottom line is that getting what we want out of life (whether it be a mansion, the perfect family or just a cold drink) requires effort and all of the procrastination in the world won't change that. All that procrastination does is make things harder for you when you eventually get around to doing the work anyway. For example, if you procrastinate on getting started on your diet, does it make it any easier when you eventually start? Of course not. In fact, if you gain weight while you procrastinate, then it only means that you have that much more weight to lose when you eventually start.

While avoiding procrastination seems like a very simple and straightforward concept, it is nonetheless crucial. In my view, the reason that many people don't reach their goals isn't because they lack intelligence, skill, talent or even money. The biggest reason for failure is that many people never get out of the starting blocks into the race of life. They *mean* to get going "one of these days" but they procrastinate on actually taking those painful first steps.

Remember only the things we have not yet begun seem out of reach. However, the moment you take that first step, your destination becomes more attainable. So my advice to you is to take the first step and take it quickly. We should remember Newton's first law of motion: An object at rest tends to stay at rest and an object in motion tends to stay in motion. So let's have some motion! Motion will seal your commitment to achieve your goals. Even if your first step seems small, it will be your most important step because it points you in the direction of your goal. Keep in mind a little progress is still progress. So keep moving, step by step, inch by inch, and sooner or later you will reach your destination.

CHAPTER 5

Your Energy

"Daddy!" squeals Mia as I walk through the door. Without taking off my coat, I kiss Wifey and then pick up my one-year-old daughter. "How is Daddy's little girl?" And with that, I raise her tiny body above my head as she grins with delight. I then give her a few more "up highs," a few airplane spins and a few "tickly-wigglies."

Within a few minutes, I start to get a little tired and decide to move our father-bonding activities to the couch. I bounce her on my knee and tickle her feverishly while Wifey admonishes, while holding our youngest daughter Sydnee, "Dion, you're going to tire Mia out!" However, Wifey has nothing to be concerned about because Mia isn't the one getting "pooped," Daddy is the one running out of steam. Within 20 minutes, I gently tell Mia that, "Daddy needs a little rest" and sadly, our bonding time is over. Pretty pathetic, huh?

This is all the more sad because I spent that whole day looking forward to spending "quality time" with her. As a speaker, I do a lot of traveling and therefore, I really appreciate every moment I get to spend with my little girl. In fact, that very day, while sitting through meetings, talking on conference calls and wading through traffic, I kept thinking, "I can't wait to get home to Mia." So why was our time cut short? Simply put, because I didn't have the energy to play with her.

Have you ever had a similar experience? Sure, you have. You

were excited to go out on a "date" with your spouse or significant other. All day long, you kept thinking, "I can't wait until tonight." However, after working a full day, wading through traffic, stopping at the market and picking up the dry cleaning, you walked through the door and said, "Honey, would you mind if we stayed in and watched a movie tonight?"

Or perhaps, after weeks (or months) of procrastinating, you finally decided that "this weekend" would be the weekend that you tackled that messy closet of yours. You were determined to finally be able to see the floor of your closet again. You even began to fantasize about all of the lost "treasures" awaiting you—your lucky shirt, that pair of suspenders that you can't seem to find anywhere, the left member of your favorite pair of shoes. In fact, if you worked your way through the closet fast enough, you were going to even start cleaning out your garage. Yet, despite your best intentions, you spent the better part of Monday morning wading through the sea of clothes on your closet floor looking for a clean pair of socks.

What happened? Well, if you are like most of us, the answer is that you ran out of gas. You didn't have the energy to follow through on your well-intentioned plans. The simple truth is that even the best plans won't work, if you won't work. You can have all of the skill, talent and desire in the world but they are worthless if you don't have the energy to act on them. Without the perquisite of energy, all of your dreams for a better future are just that—*dreams*.

To turn our dreams into reality, we must take action; oftentimes, massive action. We can't fool ourselves into thinking we can accomplish big things when we only have a little bit of energy. Therefore, before we get started on a goal, we should give some careful thought as to the amount of energy required for the task and whether we currently have that amount of energy or whether we can somehow acquire it.

After all, would you embark on a cross-country trip with just a quarter tank of gas? Probably not. You would likely fill your tank before you got started. And you would also make sure that you brought along enough money to refill your tank several more times along the way. Well, the same thought process is required when you take a journey on the path of personal development. Here are a few tips to help you find more energy.

Be Aware of Your Energy Patterns

When assessing your energy, one of the first things to do is to look at your daily energy patterns. For most of us, our level of energy doesn't stay constant throughout the day. Some people are "morning people." Their minds and bodies are freshest first thing in the morning. However, by late afternoon and evening, they start to lose steam. Other people take a while to "heat up" but by the afternoon, they are cooking! And then others are night owls. They just seem to muddle through the day but when the lights go out and everyone else goes to bed, watch out! What type of person are you?

And remember, there are no "right" or "wrong" answers to this question. However, once you know the time of day you have the most energy, you can begin to schedule your most important tasks for when you are at your best. For instance, I am a morning person. In fact, on most days, I accomplish more from 5–9 a.m. than I accomplish for the entire rest of the day. For this reason, I schedule my most demanding work for the early morning hours.

On the other hand, my sister Trish is just the opposite. By her own admission, she is completely useless before noon, and she's not much better during the early hours of the afternoon. However, when the sun goes down, her energy level goes up. While the rest of the world sleeps, Trish burns the midnight oil and she gets lots of miles to the gallon this way.

Of course, you can't always choose your schedule (although you can do so more than you probably think you can). There will be times when you have to work in "off-peak" hours. For instance, although I do my best work from 5–9 a.m., I'm not able to give many speeches during this time. For some "crazy" reason, meeting planners usually schedule their keynote presentations during the lunch or dinner hours when their attendees are actually awake. Therefore, I must be able to give my best during these times.

One way that I've found to do this is to *step into the light.* Take a walk outdoors in the sun. Bright light stimulates the brain and makes us alert. Therefore, if you find that your energy is dropping, take a quick 5 to 10 minute walk outdoors. And even if you are too tired to walk, then simply find a park bench and sit in the sun for a while. On rainy days, substitute incandescent light for sunlight. Sure, sunlight is better but any bright light can give you a quick energy boost.

One recent study showed that *listening to music is an effective way to improve your energy.* This is particularly true of the toe-tapping, rhythm variety of music. Therefore, you can always increase your current energy level by listening to your favorite music—the music that makes you want to jump up and start dancing. As the blood starts pumping, you will have a renewed sense of energy.

Be Aware of What You Are Eating

Another major *determinant of your energy level is your diet.* In one sense, this is fairly obvious. After all, the food you take into your body is the fuel your body burns to create energy. According to Dr. Janet Taylor, "there are three main sources of energy from food—carbohydrates, protein and fat. You need different combinations of all of these to stay healthy and grow. And depending on what your main need is, there are different ways to use the food that you eat to your advantage. And who doesn't need an advantage?"

Of course, there are many books on the subject of nutrition so I will leave it to you and your physician to discover the best diet for you. However, regardless of your individual dietary needs, there are a few strategies that we all could use to get the most out of our bodies.

Although we've all grown up hearing that breakfast is the most important meal of the day, how many of us act accordingly? In the frenzy of getting dressed, preparing the kids for school and navigating rush hour traffic, many people skip breakfast altogether. You don't need to be a brain surgeon to realize that this may not be the smartest move in the world.

After all, our bodies have been deprived of food for the last 6 to

51

8 hours. Yet, all of that time, they have been burning fuel in the process of rejuvenating them for another day of action. Then we wake up in the morning and immediately, our bodies start racing at full steam but without any new fuel to burn. Is it any surprise that many people find themselves at work at 11 a.m. wondering if it's time to go home yet? They have simply run out of gas.

Therefore, one of the best things you can do for your energy level is to eat a *balanced* breakfast. Of course, the key word here is "balanced." Contrary to popular belief, two crème-filled doughnuts is not a balanced breakfast. Yes, I will admit that it's a delicious breakfast but your body can't burn "delicious." A good breakfast requires fruits, protein, calcium and fiber.

This presents a special challenge for many people because it's difficult to have a grapefruit, a piece of wheat toast, a slice of ham and a glass of milk while driving to work. For this reason, we often resort to "quickie" treats like Pop-Tarts and cereal bars. However, when we try to take a shortcut with our diets, it's our bodies that usually end up broken down on the side of the road.

Sadly, breakfast isn't the only meal that we try to cram in. We have become a nation of "drive-through eaters." The problem, however, is that most fast food is high in fat and salt and sugar, which means that it provides very little in way of usable fuel. Furthermore, your fries are not the only thing being "super-sized," you are! Therefore, if you *must* eat fast food, try to stay away from the greasy burgers, oily fries and sodas and instead, try ordering the salads and drinking water. Most fast food restaurants now offer choices from a healthy menu so why not take advantage of it?

According to [Bonci], "a shortage of fluids is a major reason people feel tired a lot. If you are low on fluids, your body goes into overdrive trying to hydrate itself." As a result, less energy is available to you to mow your lawn, run a mile or give an energetic sales presentation because your body is consuming most of its energy trying to create hydration. Therefore, perhaps the easiest energy-enhancing thing you can do for yourself is to drink plenty of water. sixty-four ounces of water a day is what is recommended by most doctors.

Obviously, you should feel free to cut back on the size of your portions and make healthier eating choices but *beware of diets that dramatically decrease your caloric intake.* They will cause your body to go into an energy rationing mode. In short, your body will say, "Hey! At this rate, we are going to run out of fuel. We need to cut out some of these non-essential activities to make sure that we have enough energy for respiration, circulation and digestion." If you've ever been on such a diet, you probably experienced just this kind of reaction. After a few days of starving yourself, you probably noticed that you had just enough energy to wake up in the morning, limp through your day and crawl back into bed at night. This was your body's effort to conserve energy until you came to your senses and started eating again.

Be Aware Of What Is Eating You

As you can see, what you eat will have a major impact on your energy level. In addition, your energy level will be greatly impacted by what's eating you. By that, I mean that stress can zap your physical and mental energy. We've all experienced this kind of energy drain. We had a particularly difficult day at work or with the kids and by the evening, we were simply exhausted. It takes every bit of our remaining strength to climb into bed.

Therefore, if you want to conserve some energy for what really matters, you must learn to control your stress levels. While this may be easier said than done, it is possible. One way to limit your stress is to take the advice of Dr. Richard Carlson: "Don't sweat the small stuff... and it's all small stuff." When you think about it, there are only a handful of things that would constitute a "real" problem in your life, such as you or a loved one becoming stricken with a serious illness or being grievously injured. Everything else really is "small stuff." However, for some reason, we seem to make these small potatoes into the main course. We allow ourselves to become stressed out by clients, coworkers and even complete strangers who cut us off in traffic. It simply isn't worth it.

The other way we allow ourselves to become stressed out is by not living in the moment. As the great pastor William M. Elliot, Jr. once said, "The reason why so many of us are overwrought, tense, distracted, and anxious is that we have never mastered the art of living one day at a time. Physically, we do live one day at a time. We can't quite help ourselves. But mentally we live in all three tenses at once—past, present, and future.... And that will not work! The load of tomorrow, added to that of yesterday, carried today makes the strongest falter."

The key to avoiding this stress (and increasing your energy level) is to live one day at a time. After all, today is the only day you can spend anyway so why spend all of your mental capital on yesterday and tomorrow? Besides, all of the worry, stress and turmoil that you can muster will not do one thing to change the events of the past; nothing will. The past is just that; past. Yes, we've all made some mistakes and have suffered some hurts in the past but why ruin our present with these things?

This attitude is particularly true when faced with the troubles of tomorrow. So many of us spend so much time worrying about what tomorrow will bring. We worry about the future prospects of our company. We worry about whether interest rates will go up or whether the stock market will go down. We worry about whether our kids will get into a good college (even when they're just in pre-school). However, all of this worry does nothing but harm your present and inevitably, your future.

After all, there is only one way to ensure your future and that is to fully utilize your present. If you are worried about not having enough money to pay for your retirement, then utilize the time available today to start an investment program. Likewise, if you are worried about the future of your marriage, then utilize the time available today to build a stronger bond with your spouse. By focusing your attention on today, you can eliminate the need to worry about the future.

Of course, a country cousin to stress is boredom. Like stress, boredom will drain you of your energy. Think about it. How energized do you feel when you are bored? Not very, right? It's almost as if our brains said, "What's the use of producing energy? We're just going to be bored anyway."

One way to avoid boredom is to move your body, or in other words, get some exercise. Of course, you may be thinking that when you can barely put one foot in front of the other, the last thing you want to think about is exercise. However, it will make a world of difference in your outlook on life.

Exercise is also a great antidote for stress. Some rather dramatic changes take place in your physical body when you encounter a stressful situation. In essence, your body goes on "red alert." All battle stations are prepared for battle. As a result, your blood pressure increases to provide more blood to your muscles. In addition, your body produces adrenaline. Your whole system becomes geared to one thing—allowing you to fight or flee.

The best way to deal with this internal state of affairs is to heed your body and give it the workout it has prepared you for—take a brisk walk, jog around the block, play tennis or basketball or some other sport. Otherwise, if you do nothing, you will literally stew in your own juices. This is not good for your present energy level or your long-term health.

Another great cure to stress and boredom is to energize yourself by living with an attitude of gratitude. The simple truth is that you have a lot to be thankful for. As we discussed in the last chapter, you have so much going for you. Sadly, most of us take our blessings for granted until they are gone. We don't appreciate our "rotten job" until we get laid off. We don't appreciate our "bad kids" until they've flown the coop and gone off to college. And the list goes on and on.

The key is to find something special each day for which you can be thankful. If you are blessed with a family, friends, good health, a job, a home to live in, a car to drive and food to eat, this should be quite easy to do. However, even if you have none of the above, you can still be grateful that you are still alive and therefore, have an opportunity to make today the best day of your life.

In fact, each morning when I wake up, I roll over and look at

Wifey and say, "Today could quite possibly be the greatest day of my life. It has all the potential in the world." I strongly recommend that you develop a similar mindset because it changes your entire outlook on the day. Instead of being focused on how much you don't want to go to work or how much you'd like to sleep another hour, you train your mind to start looking for ways to make today live up to its promise. Besides, you could be right. Today could be the best day of your life. Some day has to be the best day; why not today?

CHAPTER 6

A Made-Up Mind

Do You Have a Made-Up Mind?

I was 16 years old when my mother, father, elder sister and I took a vacation not far from the White River in Little Rock, Arkansas, and stayed in a rustic cabin. One morning, my father and I decided to go fishing. So we rented a boat and took it out on the White River. It was a beautiful day. In fact, it was the kind of day that you look back fondly on 20 or even 30 years later. However, this day became quite memorable for another reason.

In a matter of minutes, the clear skies turned gray, the wind howled and it began to rain. We were unaware that a heavy storm was brewing in the area. Before long, the water became choppy and the rain pelted down upon us. It became apparent that fishing was no longer an option and we should return to the dock. As providence would have it, our wish was soon granted, but not in the way we expected. One moment, we were bobbing along in our boat toward the shore when all of a sudden the boat capsized and we were thrown into the raging water.

I do not remember the boat tipping over or even hitting the water but I do remember hearing my father yell, "Son, grab onto the boat!" As we held on to the boat for dear life, I realized we were in big trouble. By now, the swift current of the river had picked up and we were headed toward an area with many rocks jutting out of the water.

We both came to the same conclusion to head for the dock and Pop said, "Dion, can you swim to shore?"

Being young and athletic, I answered enthusiastically, "Yes!" Pop then said, "OK! You start and I will follow!"

With that, I let go of the boat and began swimming toward the riverbank. I do not remember how far it was to shore or how long it took to get there because I was concentrating on swimming through the rough water. Finally, I reached a dock on the shore. Once I had grabbed hold of the dock, I immediately turned around to reach for my father, but he was not there.

I frantically searched the surface and shouted "Dad? Dad? Can you hear me? Where are you?" Finally, I spotted him struggling in the water. My father was a large man—6' 7" and 240 pounds. In addition, it had been a long time since he had swum so far. I could see that his glasses were askew and he appeared exhausted. Upon seeing me, he raised a hand and then sank beneath the surface. I continued to shout and watch for him to surface but to no avail. Fearing the worst, I pushed off the dock and waded back into the river to find Pops. All the while, I searched frantically for any sign of him and kept calling his name, "Pops? Pops?" Then, all of a sudden, I spotted him. He was just a few feet away from me. I extended my leg and yelled, "Pops! Grab my leg!" He did and I began to tow him to shore. Once again, I put my head down and took stroke after stroke until finally, I reached the dock. We both held onto the dock, too exhausted to pull ourselves out of the water.

Fortunately, within a few minutes, a local family found us there. They had seen us out on the river and thought that we might need a hand. They helped pull us out of the water and wrapped us in blankets until local officials arrived and took us back upstream to be reunited with our family.

Over the years, I have thought about that day many times. In fact, I often tell this story in my speeches. I am often asked how a 16-year-old boy was able to tow himself and a fully grown man (particularly a man as tall as my father) through a raging river. The answer is simple I had a made-up mind. Losing Pops in that river on that day simply was not an option for me. I never once considered the possibility that either of us would perish in such a senseless tragedy. It simply could not happen that way.

I have come to realize that this is the key to success in any endeavor in life—to have a made-up mind. If you develop a "do or die" attitude about your goals in life, you will not fail. It is really that simple. A made-up mind will allow you to swim against the current of life, whether it is the current of public opinion, the current direction of the economy or any other impediment that stands between you and your objective.

Of all the principles I will share with you in this book, this is perhaps the single most important principle. Your mind will serve as the basis for any success you attain in life. In fact, your mind not only determines how well you will live but in some cases, it will determine if you live at all.

Over the last century, doctors have discovered that one of the most significant factors in determining a patient's prognosis is his or her mind-set. Patients who think they will survive outlive those who think they will die. This is why we often observe the placebo effect. In these cases, patients are given drugs with no real medicinal qualities. However, they are told that the drugs will cure them. In an amazing number of cases, these patients become "cured." In fact, the placebo effect is so common that all major drug trials now include a placebo group whose results are tested against the patients receiving "real" drugs.

Of course, the process works in reverse as well. In addition to the placebo effect, there is also a *nocebo* effect. In this case, a patient will become ill after being misdiagnosed with a disease. Even though the patient is perfectly healthy, his mindset in an illness will begin to manifest the symptoms of the disease in his body. One documented study of the nocebo effect involved 57 high school boys in Japan. Each of the boys had, in the past, experienced a severe reaction after coming into contact with the lacquer tree, which can cause itchy rashes much as poison oak and poison ivy do. The boys were blindfolded and the researchers brushed one arm with leaves from a lacquer tree but told the boys they were chestnut tree leaves. The researchers stroked the other arm with chestnut tree leaves but said the foliage came from a lacquer tree. Well, I think you can guess what happened. Within minutes, their *minds* were convinced they had been exposed to the poisonous tree and they began to react, turning red and developing a bumpy, itchy rash, while in most cases, the arm that had contact with the actual poison did not react. Therefore, as you can see, your mind is powerful. It is often more powerful than the "facts."

One way to enforce your made-up mind is to take away the possibility of failure. That is exactly what happened that day on the White River. While some people would call my actions on that afternoon heroic, nothing could be further from the truth. A hero is someone like a fireman who *voluntarily* rushes into a burning building to save a complete stranger with full knowledge of the danger. I did not have a choice. My dad was out there struggling in that water. I desperately needed him in my life (I still do) so there really was not a choice at all. The only choice was *how* to save him, not whether or not I would save him.

That is the kind of choice we should all apply to the really important goals in our lives. It is not a matter whether you will finance your non-profit organization or not, but *how* you will do it. And the same principle applies to anything you want to accomplish—buying your first home, sending your kids to college, retiring by age 50, you name it. There is real power when you take away all avenues of retreat.

In the end, the bottom line really comes down to one question: "How badly do you want it?" In sports, when the coach of the losing team is interviewed and asked why his team lost, he will invariably say, "The other team just wanted it more than we did." This is accurate more often than not. At the professional level, there is not much difference between the players in terms of talent and ability. They are all among the very best of the best in their particular sports.

And while you may not be a world-class athlete, the same principle holds true with your dream. This truth was illustrated more than two thousand years ago by Socrates. As the legend goes, one day, a devoted follower pleaded with Socrates to share with him the secret of acquiring knowledge. "This is how," Socrates said as he pushed the young man into the river and held his head under the water. Every time, the young man attempted to rise, Socrates pushed his head further into the water. After a while, the young man became frantic. He began kicking, fighting and clawing at Socrates until he was finally able to free himself and rise to the surface. As the young man stood in the river coughing and gasping for air, Socrates asked him, "When you thought you were drowning, what one thing did you want most of all?"

The young man yelled, "I wanted air!"

Socrates then smiled and said, "When you want knowledge as much as you wanted air, then you will get it!"

Well, the same is true for anything you want out of life. When you want it as much as a drowning man wants air, you'll get it.

Ask yourself; Do you have a made-up mind? In other words, are you determined to have your goals come to pass no matter what? Notice what I am not asking. I am not asking for you to make a decision to reach your goals because a decision can be changed. You can decide to do something today and decide not to do it tomorrow. What I want to know is whether your mind is made up. Is your mind fixed to accomplish this goal regardless of the obstacles in your way? It is this type of made-up mind and emotion that brings results.

Take a minute and think about the last time you truly had a made-up mind about something, anything. Remember the time when you were willing to do whatever had to be done to get the results you wanted. You knew without a shadow of a doubt that you were going to get your desired results.

Now envision that time, put yourself back in that situation, and feel, once again, the motivating power of your own made-up mind. Experience, once again, the confidence that comes with having a made-up mind to the point that nothing can stop you.

You know how powerful and energizing a made-up mind can feel, and you know the valuable results it brings. Whatever you think has a strange way of coming your way. It is almost as if your actions conform to your made up mind. So now the only thing left to do is to do it! Make up your mind that no matter what, you're going to reach your goal.

CHAPTER 7

Becoming a Goal Getter

Now that you've hopefully gotten clear on *exactly* what you want to do in life, it's time to bring it to pass. In other words, it's time to put together your master plan. Your master plan will be your step-by-step road map to success. This plan will be the culmination of all you are—your knowledge, your experience, your skills and your resources. It all begins to come together in the creation of an effective guide to help your reach your wildest dreams. Whether you realize it or not, you have spent your entire life preparing for this time. Now is your chance to put it all together.

Consider yourself ripe and ready to unleash all your true potential. Consider for a moment all you have going for you. Today you are wiser than you have ever been before, plus you posses the capability to learn more. You have a clear vision of where you have been and where you're going. You have the same 24 hours in a day as did great and successful people before you. You have skills and talents that have been untouched up to this point. You will never run out of new ideas. You are like a well of creativity that will never run dry. All that needs to be done now is to get all these great resources from within you and put them to work for you. Let's face it; all these treasures are worthless if you can't have access to them. It would be like you found a locked safe with a note telling you that the safe contains 20 million in treasures. In this case, unless the note also told you the combination to the safe, it would be virtually worthless to you. Of course, if you were determined enough to open the safe, you could try all the various combinations, but this process could take years.

Interestingly, I think this analogy best describes the situation that many people find themselves in. They have been given limitless treasures but they don't have the combination to open the "safe." Well, if this has been your problem in the past, fear no longer because I have the combination. The combination is: Write it down, Break it down, Bring it around.

Step 1. Write It Down

The first step in becoming a Goal Getter is to write down your goal. By writing down your goal, you give life to it. What could possibly constitute a better use of your time and energy than to clearly write out the desire which yearns in you? After all, your dreams and desires are your gift and they are your obligation. You must treat them with respect. One way to do this is to give them the attention they deserve by writing them down.

One helpful thing that you can do is to develop what I call a "party statement." As the name implies, a party statement allows you to express your mission to someone at a party in a quick sentence or two. My party statement when I first wanted to become a motivational speaker was: "*I am a motivational speaker who helps others overcome obstacles.*" As a result of having a party statement, you can explain to anyone you meet what you are about and what you are trying to accomplish in a matter of seconds.

By developing a party statement, you enable others to help you reach your dream. In my experience, people are generally willing and eager to help you reach your dream. However, they can't help you reach a dream that they don't know you have.

Before I had a party statement, it would be difficult to quickly inform a casual acquaintance of my desire to be a motivational speaker. For this reason, I would often not say anything about my dream at the time. Later, when I would tell them, they would say something like, "I wish I had known you were a speaker! I would have invited you to speak to our group." However, since developing a statement, I can't tell you the number of times that people have helped to put me into contact with people who could book me to speak for their groups.

Developing a party statement also has one more important benefit—you get the opportunity to say your dream out loud. In fact, this benefit of the party statement may be more valuable than any networking or referral benefit. As we discussed earlier, your mind is most influenced by the things you experience through your senses. *Thinking* that you want to be the mayor of your town is one thing but saying it is quite another. The act of saying it requires that you not only think it but that you *hear* it as well. And let's face it, if you have a big goal (and I really hope you do), you're going to need every advantage you can get to make it happen.

So what will be your party statement?

(Write your "Party Statement" here)

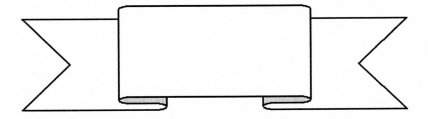

Step 2. Break It Down

The second step after writing it down is to break it down.

One thing that will keep you moving forward is to break your goal into smaller chunks. After all, this is how an ant eats an elephant... one bite at a time. And this is how you will achieve your goal... one chunk at a time. . In fact, you've successfully used this strategy hundreds of times in your life. For example, have you ever put together a jigsaw puzzle? If so, then you know that it doesn't take a "genius" to do it. What it does require is the patience to work piece by piece through the puzzle. One by one, the pieces start to come together and before long, the picture starts to come into focus.

The same is true for your dream. You start with scattered pieces to your dream and a vision of what the end result should look like. And one by one, you start putting the pieces together until the picture of your reality starts to match your vision. It's really that simple and we *know* this to be true. However, we allow ourselves to be fooled by the myth of "talent." We say, "Well, yes, that will work for her because she has talent but I'm not as gifted."

Talent has very little to do with it. For instance, in the previous example, a talent for puzzle building will allow you to finish your puzzle faster than another person but everyone can build a puzzle. The same is true with building a business, writing a book or learning to play the piano. If you just take it piece by piece, you *will* succeed.

Success in any area of life is usually the result of very mundane activities done consistently. For instance, the successful entrepreneur builds his business by consistently doing "simple" things like making phone calls, writing letters, balancing the books, answering e-mail, etc.

In fact, even in the speaking business, the main determinant of success and failure is not talent. Sure, it helps to have a melodious voice. And yes, it's great if you can make people laugh, tell fascinating stories or otherwise entertain people. However, talent is not the key to success in this business (or any other). The most successful people in this business are the ones who consistently do the little things—show up on time, send "Thank you" notes, return phone calls, write letters, etc. Success is simply a matter of doing the little things over and over again until they turn into something big.

Therefore, let's take a moment to start constructing your goal into something big. The first step is to lay out all the pieces on the table. Have you ever tried putting together a puzzle with all the pieces still in the box? It's frustrating, right? One reason for this frustration is because you keep picking up the same pieces over and over. However, once you lay out all the pieces, you have a greater sense of clarity. The same is true here.

Therefore, I suggest you take a piece of paper write down everything that comes to mind that you need to reach your goal. Does your goal require that you possess a special skill or advanced degree? Does your goal require a certain amount of money? If so, write down the *exact* amount? Does your goal require you to have contacts with certain people? If so, who?

The key here is to be as specific as possible. For instance, writing down that you need to be "smarter" doesn't have a whole lot of power. How much smarter? As measured by whom? On the other hand, if you write down that you need a master's degree in anthropology, then you have a concrete task to accomplish.

Also, if you need certain equipment like a truck or a computer, then list it *specifically*. After all, there's a big difference between needing a pick-up truck and a Hummer. The same is true with computers. And also, don't forget the accessories. Do you also need a monitor, printer, scanner, copier, fax machine, etc.? It's important to get an accurate picture of *exactly* what you need to accomplish your goal.

For example, if your goal is to start a consulting business, your list might look something like this:

Incorporation
Letterhead
Business cards
Custom logo
Computer
Printer
Business Line
Fax machine
Bank account
Brochure
Mailing list
Wall Street Journal Subscription
PO Box
Write a book

$25,000 operating capital
Hire a bookkeeper
Find a mentor
Write a newspaper column

Next, arrange your list in order of priority. This can often be tricky because the natural inclination is to do the easiest things first. And certainly there is some wisdom to this idea because you gain momentum by getting things done. However, there are some things that must be done before others. Just as when you bake a cake, there is an order to the ingredients. So, for instance, using the list above, it would be a lot easier to open a bank account than to form your corporation. However, your bank won't open an account for your business until after the corporation is officially formed. Therefore, some steps must be accomplished before others, even if they are more difficult to accomplish.

Also, some steps require a greater lead time than others. Therefore, as a general rule, those steps should be initiated first. This allows you to get those actions in process while you move on to other things. For example, your phone company may take up to a week or two to install your new phone line. As a result, you may want to contact them before you're ready to start your business so that you won't have to sit around waiting for your phone line to be installed at a later date.

In situations where the proper order still isn't clear, I suggest you ask yourself, "What is the most important thing to do next?" Perhaps, a better way to ask this question is, "If I could only do one more thing on this list, what would it be?" Once you've made your decision, you then decide what is next. Repeat that process with the rest of the list.

Finally, once you've listed your tasks and ordered them by level of priority, the final step is to set a deadline for each task. While this is a good idea for all tasks, it's critical for those tasks that are most difficult to accomplish. For example, let's suppose one of your tasks is to buy a new computer. However, at present, you don't have the money to buy a new computer. In this case, it's important to put a deadline of getting the money for a new computer. A deadline creates a sense of urgency. Without a deadline, we all have a tendency to put things off indefinitely. Therefore, when faced with a decision about whether to spend your money on something frivolous or save it for the computer, you are much more likely to make the "right" decision if you're trying to meet a deadline. Otherwise, you might say, "Hey, I'll have a little fun now. There's always time to buckle down and save for a computer later."

Also, when setting your deadline, it's important to be firm but realistic. When you set unrealistic deadlines, you diminish the effect of the deadline. It becomes like not having a deadline at all. It is always a good idea to give yourself enough time to reach your deadline. By doing so you build confidence to keep moving forward and reaching other deadlines.

Step 3. Bring It Around

The third step in this three-step plan is to bring it around. In other words, it is now time to complete the task you have listed. Confucius once said, "A journey of a thousand miles begins with a single step." So the first thing to do is to make a step. You can't reach a really big goal all at once just as you can't drive across the country in a single day. But what you can do is to keep moving forward. Remember a little progress is still progress. The key here is to keep moving towards your goal.

The best way to do this is to complete each task on your list one at a time. Sometimes it seems overwhelming when you look at the long list of things that you need to do. By choosing just one thing to do at a time, you will be able to build momentum to do the others. Even if you think you're taking only a small step. That small step you take will get you closer to your goal and in time you will get where you want to be. It is just a matter of concentrating on one task at a time.

By the way, this is a very important skill to develop—the ability to work on one task to the exclusion of all others until it's completed. A half-done task is really not done at all. It has no value to you until it's completed. For that reason, you should try to complete one task and then move on to the next one. Remember, it's better to complete one task than to leave twenty tasks half-done.

It is also important to note that you are not going to reach all your goals or complete all your steps by bedtime. What you can do is to commit yourself to completing something on your list each day. You will soon find that there is great power in crossing things off your "to do" list. You will experience a great feeling of accomplishment. By doing this, you can see for yourself that you are making progress. Even if the steps you take are small, deep down inside you will know you're closer to your goal than you were when you started out. The important thing is to stay disciplined, focused, and committed to make progress daily.

One of the greatest skills I have ever learned is how to get focused for whatever task lies in front of me. Let's be honest, there are some days that we are not in the mood to do anything. Nevertheless things still need to be done. For this reason it is important to know how to get yourself motivated and focused to complete the task that needs to be done. Imagine you had an interview with an organization you have been waiting to hear back from. Unfortunately you did not get much sleep the night before and quite frankly you are having a bad day. Nevertheless your interview is in thirty minutes. Could you do it? Could you put all your problems behind you, get yourself motivated and focused to accomplish the task of nailing the interview? Those who can have a definite advantage in life over those who let their "moods" dictate their performance.

So how does one do this? How can you shake off whatever is bothering you or holding you back and get energized to be victorious? I only know of one way. Practice. Believe it or not, you have many opportunities to practice this art throughout the day. I first started doing this when I realized I was coming home grumpy from a long day at work. I did not want to take my day out on my family, so what I would do is stop at the door before I entered the house. I would then take about thirty seconds to get myself energized for my family. I would think about how excited I am to see them, how glad

I am that the work day is over, and I committed myself to bring laughter and joy out of my wife and daughters. From there, I walk through the door feeling one hundred percent better. I do the same thing for meetings, interviews, basketball games, phone calls, etc. I will admit the energy does not last forever, but neither does the task that needs to be accomplished. The important thing is that you get "up" for the task and oftentimes momentum will carry you through completion.

How many opportunities can you find in a day to get focused? Remember, the more highly focused you are, the more impressive your accomplishment will be. Those who master this skill will reach their destination much easier than those who do not.

Keep Your Eyes on the Prize

There is an old saying that states: You can't see the forest because of the trees. In other words a person can get so fixated on what makes up the forest (trees) they lose sight of the forest itself. Well the same thing is true when trying to reach our goals. We get absorbed and sometimes lost in what needs to be done we lose sight of our intended goal. And as a result, we can give up. For this reason, it is always a good idea to keep your eyes on the prize. Once you can see yourself reaching your goals and being the person you want to be, you will have a much better chance of turning your vision into a reality. In fact, without such a vision, it is very difficult (if not impossible) to reach your goal.

The importance of a clear vision of your goal is demonstrated by the example of Florence Chadwick—the first woman to swim the English Channel. For years, she trained for her historic swim. Finally, in 1952, she was ready. As she set out from France, she was full of confidence and hope. However, as she approached the coast of England, a heavy fog engulfed her and the water became increasingly cold and choppy. From a boat nearby, her mother and others began to yell out words of encouragement. They told her that she was just a few miles from the coast and that she could make it. However, Florence was exhausted and with the coastline nowhere in sight, she asked to be pulled into the boat.

Obviously, Florence was heartbroken over her failure to reach her goal. She was even more heartbroken when she learned that she was just a few hundred yards from the English coast when she quit. This is not the end of the story.

Florence decided to try again a little while later. However, this time, she developed a mental picture of the coast of England. Repeatedly, she visualized every nook and cranny of the British coastline. In fact, she could clearly see the coastline even with her eyes closed. Therefore, when she encountered the same foggy and choppy conditions on her second crossing, she didn't panic. She could mentally see her goal and so she kept swimming, becoming the first woman to swim the English Channel.

I can tell you from experience that the same thing will happen to you on your journey to your dream. There will be many days when the path ahead looks foggy and you cannot see your way clear to your goal. On those days, the only thing that will keep you from giving up and being asked to be pulled into the boat of mediocrity will be your mental image of the shore and your willingness to keep moving forward one step or stroke at a time. Just keep reminding yourself at some point success is just one step away. And before long you won't be stepping to your goal, you will be standing on it!

CHAPTER 8

3 Keys to Open Any Door

In trying to reach your goals, you are bound to run into closed doors. Doors that may read, "No Women Allowed" or "Impossible Turn Around" or "Beware of Glass Ceiling." However by using the right key at the door, you would be amazed at how many doors can open for you. In my journey to reach success I have found three keys that seem to work every time. These keys are: People, Persistence and Prayer.

First Key: People

I once knew this kid in high school who seemed to have it all. His parents gave him a new Corvette at the age of 16. He lived in the guesthouse of his parents' home (which came with its own swimming pool). He was good-looking and very talented. He was always flashing money around school and of course, women worshiped him. He seemed to have it all. One day I saw him in the school cafeteria sitting and eating all by himself. This by itself was strange. Strange not because he was by himself but strange that with so much money he was eating the school food. It's for this reason I sat next to him to ask him why he did not go out for lunch. He was looking pretty down and I soon found out why. He told me he totaled his new Corvette and he had no transportation. I told him, "Man, that's a bummer." He then told me he couldn't care less about the car.

His parents said they would get him a new one. What bothered him the most was when it happened his parents never checked to see if he was all right, never asked what happened, or even took the time to consult with him. They simply left a note on his door saying it will be replaced. This was the first time I have ever heard this guy open up like this. He went on to tell me that the only reason he got all this cool stuff was because his parents never spent time with him, so it was their way of keeping him happy. But he said he would give it all up for someone to be there for him and give him love, support and direction in life.

From this I learned *when it comes to success it is not what you have in your life but who you have in your life.* Having the right people in your corner is one of the most important keys to have when trying to reach your goals and being happy. Successful businessmen and women have known this for years. I have often heard in the business arena that your net worth will be linked to your abilities to network. Just one helpful tip from a trusted person can take years off your journey to reach success. In fact, there is a roadside sign in northern California that demonstrates this point. The sign reads: "24,956 miles to Case de Fruita… or just 4 miles if you turn around." Sometimes, you can be so close to your destination and not even know it. In those times, a helpful hint can make all of the difference. One of most popular and effective ways to foster relationships with people is to *treat everyone you meet like they are the most important person you know.* It is the "Golden Rule." Treat people like you want to be treated. By doing so, you have a chance to build relationships. Another reason we should make it a practice to do this is that oftentimes, they think they are the most important person we know anyway. Most people we meet could speak for hours about themselves and what's going on in their life. And many times they do. The reason being, they see themselves as important people, so why not treat them like they are? By doing so you will have a better chance of building some type of relationship. This is important because *people will do more for a relationship than they will for a dollar.*

Imagine how wonderful it would be to have an uncle who is a dentist, or a sister who owned a fancy restaurant. What about having a good friend who was the owner of a Lexus dealership? Wouldn't that be grand? Of course, because chances are your uncle would not charge you for dental work, nor would your sister charge you to eat at the fancy restaurant. As far as the Lexus is concerned, I am sure your good friend would at least get you the best deal possible. Why? Because people will do more for a relationship than they will for a dollar. I can't name all the times I have been able to render services from people I know that I would never be able to afford—simply because we were friends. I learned this concept from a friend in college. Our college was trying to find a speaker to come speak to the students for Charter Day for free. My friend Karen said she would ask the Rev. Jesse Jackson to come speak. Naturally, we all laughed, knowing he was too busy and too far away to come speak to a small college like ours. Besides, there was the fact that we could not afford to pay him anything. Yet, when Charter day came so did the Rev. Jesse Jackson. We were all shocked! I asked my friend Karen, "How in the world did you get Jesse Jackson to come to our school?" She said, "Easy. He is my friend!"

Take time to consider the relationships you have already established. Many times we have friends who are willing to help us reach our goals if we simply ask. This is another reason why it is so important to treat every person you meet like they are the most important person you know—because sooner or later they may be. It's very difficult to accomplish anything alone. And it is quite unnecessary, as well. There are plenty of people willing to help you if you will only ask.

Something to remember when building relationships with people is that *people will forget what you said and they may forget what you have done, but never how you made them feel.* Have you ever been upset with a person but not be able to remember why you're upset? Maybe you had an argument long ago and yet can't remember the details of the argument. Have you ever run across an old friend or somebody you have met before but you can't remember his or her name or where you met him or her or when? But what you do remember is they were friendly towards you. This same principle applies to those you may have ill feelings towards as well. We may not always remember why we avoid them, but we get a bad feeling as soon as we see them. Why is that? It is because feelings and emotions stay with us longer than memory. Therefore it is important to always try and leave a good impression or "feeling" with those you come in contact with.

I can remember going through the Chicago O'Hare airport on my way to a speaking engagement when a young man came up to me and said "D., how are you?" I had no idea who this young man was, but I did know that he must have heard me speak at his high school because high schools are the only places I tell the students to call me "D." So I quickly said. "Hey, how ya doing? I must have met you at your high school."

He said, "Yeah, I am in college now and I have you to thank for it. That talk you gave us about having what it takes to make it in college inspired me go."

I said "Wonderful. What was it that I said?" At that point he stopped, looked at the ground and all around as if he dropped the answer.

Finally, he said, "You know, D., I don't remember what you said, but I do remember leaving that place feeling like I could do it." To me, that was the best compliment I could have ever received. There is something about feelings of joy, excitement, fear and anger that we remember much better than just words and actions. Therefore, it is always a good thing to leave people feeling good about the time spent with you.

People can be a powerful source of ideas, of creativity, of business contacts and money. Generally speaking, most people are genuinely flattered when you ask for their opinion or their expertise. Most people are willing to help if they can. Where we have to be careful is to not take advantage of people. Asking someone for his or her help because you don't want to do the work yourself will not last long. People are willing to help you only if they see you are putting forth your own best effort. No one likes to be taken advantage of. Most people will not want to help you if you don't help yourself first.

One of the best ways to ask for anything from anyone is to first offer something. If you need experience in something, offer your time to volunteer. If you're asking for support, offer your support first. When you offer, you put yourself in a persuasive position. Now you are not just asking, but giving as well, which in turn is harder to turn down compared to someone just looking for handouts. The things you have to offer are priceless. Your time, your experience, your knowledge, your attention, your understanding. First find what the other person needs and before you ask for anything, offer something of value and watch the wonderful results it brings.

Take time to write down who it is that you have built relationships with who can help you reach your goal. Also take time to write down how you can help them reach theirs. By doing so, you will find yourself with a ring of keys that can help you open many doors.

In conclusion, there is one final thought concerning people I would like to leave with you. There is an old saying, "It's not what you know, but who you know that makes a difference." However, in reality it is really about *who wants to know you.* You can say that you know the president of the United States, Donald Trump or the Queen of Switzerland, but what good is that? Now imagine if these people wanted to get to know you! Imagine that you were so impacting the world that these "big" names wanted to take time out of their life to get to know you. Wouldn't that be grand? So make it your goal not just to get to know people, but be the person people would want to get to know.

Second Key: Persistence

Persistence is probably the most important quality necessary to achieve success. Yet anyone can have persistence. It is a choice you are always free to make. It requires no special skill. It is the ability to move forward regardless of obstacles, circumstances or opposing forces. Nobody knows this better than successful men, women and babies. Little babies know what they want and usually get it. Not because they are smarter than others or more talented, but because they are persistent! Likewise, successful men and women have learned how to stay persistent in order to reach their intended goal.

Everything does not always go as planned or anticipated. Persistence is the ability to continue in the face of adversity. Good or bad ideas are proven good or bad through the failure or success of our efforts. Even good ideas cannot be proven without a persistent effort to implement them. For example, most people have heard about Thomas Edison's odyssey in inventing the incandescent light bulb. In short, Edison is reported to have tried more than 10,000 times before finally succeeding. As the story is told, each time Edison failed to produce a fiber that conducted electricity, he threw it out of the window. Within a year, this pile of fibers reached the second floor of his laboratory.

Often, this story is retold as the ultimate example of persistence. And it certainly is important for that reason. However, there is another important thing to learn from this story. Edison was not only persistent but he was also methodical. Each time, he tried a method that didn't work, he recorded his results so that he would know not to try that method again. He didn't just keep trying the same thing over and over again and hoping for a different result. If he had done so, we might all be sitting in the dark today. According to Edison, genius is one percent inspiration and ninety-nine percent perspiration.

Edison varied his approach each time until he finally succeeded, and so should you. For example, if you've just started in sales and are having trouble making the first sale, then you must keep trying. However, you must also vary your approach. You can't just call on the same prospect with the same presentation every day and expect a different result. Try contacting new prospects and with these prospects, vary your presentation. It's important to keep trying but it's equally important to change your approach.

Our persistence is directly linked to our desire. Our degree of desire will determine how persistent we will be. If we want or need something bad enough, we will develop the mind-set and energy level to persevere through all the obstacles and disappointments put before us. With persistence, one small effort builds on top of the one before, until the combined force is undeniable. These efforts, strung together over time bring about outstanding results. Persistence can open up doors that you never thought were possible simply because persistence never quits.

Third Key: Prayer

The third key I have found to open doors is prayer. Some may argue that this third key should have been the first, while others may argue it is not a key at all. However I have found out that there will be some doors that are shut so tight that the only way they will open is through divine intervention. In other words, you have to be able to call on a greater assistance than yourself, your friends and your persistence. For some this may sound ridiculous, but for those who have experienced this type of help before, they know the difference it can make. The religious community has known this for years. However, as of late, many in the medical and scientific world have come to grips with this reality.

In Colorado Springs, Colorado, Dr. Arnold Ahnfeldt was confronted with a difficult case involving a hairdresser who faced amputation of her severely infected thumb. After neither medication nor surgery had stemmed the infection, Ahnfeldt posed a somewhat novel alternative.

"We've reached the limits of our abilities," Ahnfeldt recalls telling the attending physician. "I think we ought to include God here." Though the older doctor was skeptical, he agreed to join Ahnfeldt and pray with the patient the night before the scheduled amputation. The next morning, doctors found that the infection had dramatically improved. Amputation was no longer necessary—a development Ahnfeldt considered "a miracle."

Ahnfeldt's philosophy is apparently being shared by more and more doctors. Not only are physicians praying with patients, but researchers studying how prayer affects healing have also found— somewhat amazingly—that in most cases it helps people get better. Those developments are part of what could be called a spiritual awakening in the nation's medical profession. Even the esteemed Harvard Medical School holds a regular conference on spirituality and medicine, and many more teaching hospitals are falling in step.

The strange thing about this key is either you believe it or you don't. Once again, it's your "belief" that will make the difference. I only have to look a few years back to be convinced that prayer is a key like none other. I mentioned earlier in this book about my awful experiences in the Army. What I failed to mention was how I cut a four year enlistment into four weeks. I can't say this is one of my proudest moments of my young life but it does make a good case for the power of prayer.

Anybody who ever enlisted in the army knows you just can't ask to be excused when you have had enough. And although I had tried to make the best of the situation, I knew, deep down inside, this is not where I was suppose to end up. To make matters worse, I was assigned to Fort Benning, Georgia, the home of the Air Rangers. I was being trained to be a paratrooper until one day, someone noticed the scars on my legs from my childhood operations. The Army brass became concerned that perhaps my legs were not strong enough for this type of duty. As a result, my continuation with boot camp was delayed while Army doctors ran a battery of tests on my legs.

In the meantime, I was assigned to be the personal errand boy for a sergeant by the name of Holmes. My daily tasks consisted of fetching his meals, cleaning his toilets and doing anything else that he desired for me to do on a particular day. In essence, I felt like I was a slave with polished shoes and a crew cut.

Needless to say, I quickly became despondent about my place in the Army; so much so that I began to desperately seek ways out of the service. One day, I became engaged in a conversation with an enlisted man who told me that there were only a few ways he knew of to get out of the Army: (1) suicide, (2) mental illness, (3) being gay or (4) a major injury. While the first and third options were simply out of the question for me, I began acting strangely in an effort to demonstrate my ever-increasing insanity. Unfortunately, the psychiatrist saw through my ploys and refused to take the bait.

Likewise I tried complaining about my legs, but that only got me in rehab.

At that point, I was left with only one option—prayer. I reported to Sergeant Holmes one morning like I always did and he ordered me to clean his toilets like he always did. While on my hands and knees cleaning the toilet I began to pray in earnest and in doing so, I began to develop a strategy for what I was going to do with my life after getting out of the Army. I decided that I would return to Texas and enroll in Huston-Tillotson College so that I could better prepare myself for the employment market.

Shortly thereafter, my prayers were answered. Within 24 hours Sergeant Holmes asked me what I wanted to do with my life. I told him my plans to go to college. He then said, "OK, Dion, I will sign an honorable discharge for you and send you on a bus back to Texas. And sure enough, just seven days later, I was on a bus back home, discharged from the Army and ready to tackle the challenges of college life. In the end, you could say, I tried to use all three keys to open this door, but in the end only one came through for me. Prayer.

CHAPTER 9

Turning Obstacles
into Opportunities

At the beginning of my speaking career, one of my first engagements was in the Chicago area. I flew into Chicago the night before the engagement. At the airport, I rented a car and drove to my hotel. I left the car with the valet and proceeded to check in and get a much needed night's rest. The next morning, I felt rested and rejuvenated and ready to take on the world.

My speech that day was outside of the city limits, so I decided to leave a little early to give myself plenty of time to find the venue. I retrieved my car from the hotel valet and I was off to my speech. To get myself in the right frame of mind, I flipped on the radio. However, I soon noticed that the radio station had been changed from the station I was listening to the night before. My immediate thought was, "I can't believe the valet guy had the nerve to change my station."

Well, to make matters worse, not only had he changed my station but he had changed all of the stations I'd pre-programmed into the radio when I rented the car at the airport. I thought that this was rather peculiar behavior for the valet at a reputable hotel but decided that I wasn't going to dwell on it, since I had a big speech to deliver.

However, I wasn't able to put it completely out of my mind

because a few miles down the road, I noticed that I only had half a tank of gas remaining, despite the fact that the tank was full when I rented the car. I knew that the drive from the airport to the hotel didn't take that much gas and I started to become angry. I surmised that the hotel's valets had taken my rental car out for a joy ride while I slept that night.

I decided that I was going to have a good, long talk with the hotel management about the scandalous behavior of their parking attendants when I returned to the hotel that afternoon. However, soon my anger turned to horror as I realized that I had left my wallet in the glove department of the car the night before. I quickly opened the glove compartment and sure enough, my wallet was gone. Now, this was really too much. I was livid!

Just then, I came upon a toll booth. Realizing that I didn't have my wallet, I started to get a little nervous because I didn't have any money to pay the toll. Desperately, I checked the ashtray and there was enough money there to pay the toll. Well, at least, *something* had gone in my favor that morning.

As I continued to drive down the road and reflect on the events of the last 24 hours, I realized that something wasn't right. I decided to take another look in the glove compartment to look at my rental agreement but it was also gone. However, in its place, I found the registration for the car. As I scanned the registration, it hit me – this was not my rental car. This car actually belonged to another guest of the hotel.

That explained why the radio was programmed to the wrong stations. That explained the disappearance of my wallet and the existence of spare change in the ashtray. I began to realize that I had never gotten a good look at my rental car because I had picked it up the night before, so I didn't notice that anything was wrong when the valet brought me the wrong car.

At this point, I had an interesting dilemma on my hands. I could return the car to the hotel immediately, but that would mean that I would miss my speaking engagement. Or I could continue on my journey and deal with the car mix-up upon returning to the hotel. I chose the latter course of action and drove to the venue of my speaking engagement.

After giving the speech, I decided that I had better return this car to its rightful owner. So I drove back to the hotel, only to find several police cars waiting at the hotel. As soon as I stepped out of the car, one of the parking attendants pointed to me and the police immediately descended upon me. As you can imagine, I had a difficult time explaining to them that I hadn't purposely stolen the car.

As I tried to explain the situation and as the officers talked with the parking attendants, I became involved in a conversation with one of the officers. He inquired as to what I was doing in Chicago and I told him that I had come to town to deliver a speech. He asked about the topic and I explained that I was a motivational speaker. The officer's eyes lit up as he began to tell me that he belonged to a group that was looking for a speaker and he asked if I'd be willing to address his group on a future trip.

In the end, the mix-up was finally cleared up and I wasn't arrested or charged with stealing the car. Even better, I was able to book a speech with the officer's group. Furthermore, that speech led to other speeches, which were very helpful in getting my fledgling career off the ground. And all of this resulted from a situation that could have had terrible consequences for me.

From this incident, I learned that our greatest opportunities often flow from obstacles. There are some obstacles on that path from where you are now to where you want to go and that these obstacles are actually blessings in disguise.

If you want to achieve true success, you have to realize there will be obstacles in your path. I have yet to meet or read about a successful person who hasn't had to overcome obstacles and if I were you, I wouldn't expect to be the first. It is important to remember that great accomplishments often come as a direct result of challenges and obstacles. People just like you have overcome obstacles that seemed impossible to overcome—yet, with the right attitude, a willing heart and a little faith they have turned their obstacles into opportunities and stumbling blocks into stepping stones. There is no greater way to build confidence than to look for these types of challenges. The key is to change your attitude from "Why me?" to "Wow, me!" This is only possible, however, when you recognize the hidden opportunities in your obstacles.

So how does this happen? How does a person turn an obstacle into an opportunity? The first thing to consider when turning obstacles into opportunities is your attitude. Remember the old saying: Life is 10% what happens to me and 90% how I react to it. Your attitude and actions when things go wrong will determine how quickly things turn around and go right for you. The sooner you can change your attitude from "Why me," to "Wow, me!" the faster you will recognize there are hidden opportunities in obstacles. Anyone can be positive when things are going right. The real key to success is to remain positive when things don't go as you planned.

What is it that has held you back from accomplishing your goal in the past? What do you anticipate being in the way in the future? By anticipating these "hidden opportunities" we can better prepare for them. Though there will be obstacles in your way, I promise there will be more opportunities than obstacles. Oftentimes your obstacles are your opportunities. It is just a matter of recognizing them when they come along. Many times, these obstacles are necessary to make us reach our full potential. For instance, oftentimes, when we think of great entrepreneurs, we think of fearless titans of industry who bravely face the unknown and forge ahead without a trace of fear. However, very often, this isn't the case at all. They aren't men and women who chased down their destinies but instead, in many cases, their destinies chased them down.

Just the other day I went to the gym to lift weights and play a little round ball. As I was walking to the gym I ran across a friend of mine who I had not seen in about three months. I know him only as JP. JP used to be what we called a gym rat. In other words, he was always at the gym doing something. Running, lifting, playing basketball or on the treadmill. When I saw him, I asked him if he was going to play basketball today. He then told me why he could not play and why I had not seen him in a while. He told me he was in a terrible bike crash. He was knocked unconscious. He broke bones in his face, his teeth were knocked out and his nose and jaw were both fractured and broken. He went on to tell me that he had not eaten anything solid in three months and the doctors would not let him do any type of workout because of the stress it may cause. Needless to say, JP seemed a little depressed.

After he told me the story, I looked at him and said with great enthusiasm, "What an awesome opportunity!" You can imagine the look that he gave me.

"What are you talking about?" he said.

I told him what a great opportunity to accomplish other major things in his life he usually didn't find the time to do because he was always at the gym. By this time, his expression went from confused to enlightened. I went on. "Think about it," I said. "I am sure you have books to read, relationships to work on, and other goals you know you need to accomplish but have not because of all the time you spend here at the gym." He then began to agree with what I said.

He said "You know, that's true." Although he did not share with me what those things were, I could tell he truly understood my point. In a matter of minutes, JP had a change of attitude and as a result was able to turn an obstacle in his life into an opportunity. You can do the same thing with the right attitude and willingness to look at things from a positive perspective.

Let's test your ability to find opportunities in the midst of obstacles: My Wifey has two goals this year. Lose weight and save money. She will be the first to admit she has a sweet tooth and loves to shop. She knows the holidays are upon us. Thanksgiving, Christmas, and New Years. She sees all kinds of obstacles in her way. First of all, during the holiday season our family loves to get together, like most, and eat. We are talking turkey, ham, candied yams, pies, stuffing, and the works. This no doubt is a weight-watcher's biggest challenge. Then if that was not tough enough, it's during this time of year that everything goes on sale! Wifey loves a good sale and strolling through the mall. Clearly, Wifey has obstacles in her way this holiday season. Or does she? Maybe what she really has are some awesome opportunities. Before you read on, take a moment and test your skills in finding opportunities hidden in obstacles. Re-read Wifey's predicament and see how many "opportunities" you are able to come up with.

Obstacles in your Path	Hidden Opportunities

How did you do? Were you able to find some "hidden opportunities" for Wifey? They are not always easy to find. That's why they are called "hidden." However they are always present. Let's take a look at some of the hidden opportunities of the holiday season.

If there is one thing almost everyone has when it comes to reaching a goal, it is a critic. **What a perfect opportunity to prove to the critics you are for real!** You can take the holiday meal and show others that you are serious about your goal. Instead of grabbing a normal size plate like everyone else, you grab a smaller plate. This alone will raise some eyebrows. And while others offer you a larger plate, you can back up your words with action when you tell them you don't need to eat that much.

The second opportunity that waits is the **opportunity to build self confidence.** If you can make it through the holidays without breaking your diet, you know you can do it all year long. Your confidence and possibilities for yourself will be endless! There is no secret formula for confidence. Confidence is a direct result of meeting challenges. And trust me, confidence is worth its weight in gold. When you are confident in yourself and your abilities, anything and everything is possible! But confidence cannot be created out of nothing. Try to do that and you'll only get arrogance, a poor substitute which crumbles at the first tough challenge.

Now, let's consider Wifey's love for shopping during the holidays when her goal is to save money. Another great opportunity! Not only does Wifey have the opportunity to build more self confidence, but she also has a great opportunity to gain something that is not possible to gain through shopping. Let me explain. Like most "shop-a-holics," Wifey has more clothes and things than she needs. So this season, she decided to go through her two closets full of clothes and **find what can she do without** and help someone in need. And amazingly enough, she was able to find bags full of gifts that **she can give to someone who is in need**. She was also able to find good things she forgot she had—and some with receipts and tags still intact. As a result, she was able to **return many items for**

something new. She was also able to **make room for new things** and **eliminate the hidden guilt she had concerning having to many unused items**. She was able to help out others in need which **gave her a feeling of warmth and fulfillment greater than going shopping**. Wow! Look at all the opportunities she had that did not cost her one cent. The most important of these things is confidence. Confidence gives you a valuable sense of satisfaction. It will give feelings of being effective and it will encourage you to tackle new challenges in order to get new accomplishments. Soon this confidence will get you in the habit of achieving and will demand you to expect the best of yourself. So don't run from your challenges but seek them out, welcome them with open arms. With obstacles and challenges come the opportunity to instill within yourself something money can't buy. The wealth of confidence that lies hidden inside of you.

Sometimes in our own lives, we need to build canals to cut through the obstacles that keep us from our goals. For example, if you have a problem with your temper, you might find yourself continuously having problems with the people in your life, whether co-workers or loved ones. Now, you can try to resolve this problem by hopping from relationship to relationship and job to job until you find the person who "understands" you or you can take care of your temper once and for all by getting some counseling. It's your choice, but I believe that life is too short to spend years adrift at sea when you can create a shortcut by just digging a little deeper.

Don't always look for the easiest, least challenging course, because often it leads to the hardest life. So start making life better for yourself by embracing the challenges and the confidence that can come from working to overcome them. Never make excuses for your shortcomings. A wise man once told me, "If you keep arguing for your limitations you will keep them." Never accept limitations and hindrances as they are, but, rather, convert them into occasions for success.

Are you going through a major obstacle in your life right now? If so, ask yourself the question: "Where's the hidden opportunity here?" Take time to write down the obstacles you have now. Reflect on past obstacles that still hold you back and anticipate future obstacles. Knowing that you may not be able to identify them all and that there will be some lurking around the corner, by reducing the ones you are aware of and by preparing your mind to turn them into opportunities you will find those things that used to trip you up will now lift you up!

Take a moment and list all the obstacles you face now in trying to reach your goals. Then take time to list all the opportunities you can find.

CHAPTER 10

How to Get Up When You Want to Give Up

As you can see, there will be many obstacles in your path to success. Yet, many of these obstacles can be blessings if you just see them in the proper light. In the last chapter, we discussed how obstacles can be opportunities for future success. In this chapter, I want to show you how to get up when you want to give up. The simple truth of the matter is that you can never lose so long as you refuse to give up.

For this reason, it's important to learn to include one very important word into your vocabulary—the word "yet."

"Yet" is a powerful word. It implies that whatever difficulty you happen to be facing is temporary. And this is really true. You aren't married *yet*. You haven't secured the financing for your business *yet*. You haven't developed all of the skills necessary to excel in your chosen profession *yet*. You haven't learned to effectively communicate with your spouse and children *yet*. You haven't lost weight or quit smoking *yet*.

Remember, it doesn't matter where you start. What matters is where you finish. I started out as a pigeon-toed kid who could barely walk. I finished as a college athlete. I started out as a tongue-tied young man who couldn't even answer a single question in class. At present, I make my living traveling the country speaking to business and civic groups. And I dare think that I'm not finished *yet*. I am excited about the possibilities for my future and you will be too once you understand the power of "yet."

In fact, Christopher Columbus's discovery of the New World was made possibly by the use of the word "yet." As you can imagine, very few people believed in Columbus's vision that the world was round. Everything about their experience told most people of the time that the world was flat. Therefore, when Columbus sat sail on his fateful voyage, most people thought he, and most members of his crew, were going on a "fool's errand."

Well, after spending months sailing west in the Atlantic Ocean without even a hint of land in sight, Columbus's crew grew discouraged. This discouragement soon turned into restlessness, which was quickly transforming into mutiny. To quell the oncoming uprising, Columbus told his men that they just hadn't found the New World *yet* and convinced them to keep going for just three more days. Before the three days were over, the New World came into view and Columbus was proven right.

Many times in your own life, you will have to deal with a similar mutiny. Your mind will say, "You've been trying to get this non-profit started forever and you're no closer now than when you first started. Let's end this 'fool's errand.'" Or perhaps, you will have to deal with an internal mutiny about your marriage or your finances or your weight. Regardless of the issue, the key is to stave off the rebellion with "yet." Tell yourself, "I know we've been at this for a long time but we're making progress. It just hasn't come into view *yet.*"

And when all else fails and mental mutiny is at hand, make a bargain with yourself like Columbus did with his crew. Give yourself just six more months to get a recording contract or just one more year to earn your degree. This self-imposed deadline will make you more focused on your goal. And more than likely, it will buy you some time until you can see your dream in the distance.

Remember, Columbus didn't reach the New World in the three-day time period. Instead, he simply reached a point where his crew could see land. It took some additional time to reach the land but the crew didn't mind because it could see the finish line. The same thing will happen with your internal "crew." Once it can see your dream coming into focus, it will give you the extra time you need to get there.

I sincerely believe that he would have kept trying to push forward to the New World until they eventually threw him overboard. And even then, I suspect he would have tried to swim westward as far as he could swim.

Remember, with each passing day, the odds are in your favor. You are continually getting closer to what you seek and furthermore, you are getting farther away from where you started. At some point, even your mutinous thoughts will begin to realize that it's too late to head back to port. For instance, in Columbus's case, by convincing his crew to head westward another three days, he was making it much more difficult for them to ever head back to Spain.

In fact, the only way that this won't work is if you are unable to convince yourself that "yet" is true. Or, in other words, you lose your faith that you will eventually get what you want out of life. And this can happen to anyone, particularly if they encounter failure after failure. They became jaded and decide to drop out of the race of life. They quit on their dreams and more importantly, they quit on themselves. This is tragic. Yet, it can be avoided.

The important thing to remember about the race of life is that it isn't one long race. Instead, it's a series of daily races. Each day, you have a chance to be a winner. You don't have to make up all the ground you lost last week, last month or last year. Sadly, many people view life just like this so once they've fallen far enough behind, they think, "The leaders are too far ahead. I could never catch up. I might as well quit now." However, this simply isn't true. It doesn't matter where you finished in the race yesterday. What matters is where you are going to finish today and tomorrow and the coming days, weeks, months and years.

You can do the same thing. If you lost in the battle to control your weight in the past, today is a new day. All of the past failed diets are just that—in the past. Today is a new opportunity for you to win. And if you don't win today, guess what? That's right. You start again tomorrow and the next day and the next day. Each day, you simply tell yourself that you haven't lost weight *yet*. The same thing applies to every other area of life. Your past defeats have nothing to do with what you can accomplish today and the day after that and the day after that. Each day provides a new opportunity for you to win.

It's important to keep trying but it's equally important to change your approach. By doing so, you are, in the words of John Maxwell, "failing forward." With each so-called failure, you are actually getting closer to your goal. Think of it this way. Between where you are now and where you want to be, there is a barrier—a door of sorts. This door is secured by a combination padlock. Each time, you incorrectly dial in a combination, you are one step closer to finding the combination that will open the lock and allow you to walk into your destiny. Therefore, all you have to do is to keep trying combinations, recording your results and saying to yourself, "I haven't found the right combination *yet.*"

Of course, as we discussed earlier, there are more efficient ways to get this lock open. One way is to ask someone who knows the combination because they've already walked through that door. In other words, find a mentor who is already where you want to be.

However, sometimes you may not be able to find such a person or you may be trying to walk through a door that has never been opened before by anyone. For example, Edison couldn't rely on a mentor to help him invent the incandescent light bulb because no one had ever done it before. He was the first person through that particular door, so he had to do it the hard way. Yet, even the most difficult tasks will eventually get done if you just keep failing forward.

Perhaps, the greatest example of someone who has failed forward is Abraham Lincoln. His entire life was a testament to failure, yet he ended up as one of the most successful people in history. At the age of 22, he failed in business. The next year, he ran for the state legislature and lost. The next year, he failed in business again. At the age of 26, his sweetheart died tragically, causing Lincoln to suffer a nervous breakdown. At the age of 29, he ran for the office of speaker and lost. Two years later, he was defeated in a race for the legislature.

Having failed completely in his efforts to be elected to a statewide office, he decided to run for congress at the age of 34. Guess what? He lost. Three years later, he ran for congress again and lost. The same thing happened two years later.

Unable to be elected to congress, Lincoln decided that this was a good time to fail forward again so he ran for the senate at age 46. No surprises here. He lost. The next year, he ran for vice president. He lost. And two years later, he was defeated in his second bid for the senate.

At this point, Lincoln had failed in business twice and lost *nine* elections. However, as you know, he didn't quit. Instead, he decided to fail forward again by running for the highest office in the land, President of the United States. And at the age of 51, Abraham Lincoln was sworn in as the 16th President of the United States. And the rest, as they say, is history.

In what area of your life could you learn to fail forward? How can you make your next attempt at success bigger than your previous failures?

One success can be more than enough. In fact, if you've been as lucky as I have to find the spouse of your dreams, then you already know this to be true. All the heartbreaks of the past pale in comparison to the joy of finding that special person. Once you find this person, you don't focus on who left you, cheated on you or didn't appreciate you. You couldn't care less. In fact, you're glad that they did leave you so that they made room for Mr. or Mrs. Right.

As you can see, failure can be your best friend so long as you learn to fail forward, instead of falling behind.

Finding that Second Wind

It's bound to happen. You're solidly on track, firmly moving towards your goals, and then it happens. You get distracted. Something happens and now all of a sudden you have lost a little steam. You're a bit off course, the energy is not quite what it was when you first started, and although your mind may still be made up it is a little sidetracked. Don't feel bad, it happens to everyone. I see it every year. Every January, Portland's Metropolitan YMCA is packed full of people with new fitness goals and new year resolutions. Everyone is excited and pumped because they know this is their year! Then slowly but surely as the weeks go by the YMCA becomes a little more spacious. Until finally in mid-March, the fitness race has slowed down back to faithful few. Rest assured that along the journey to success, occasionally you'll wander off in the wrong direction. You've gotten good at going through the routine, but perhaps you've lost touch with the reasons why you're doing it all in the first place. For some people they love to start things but soon after they begin they get bored with their goal or it loses its excitement. It's during times like these you should stop for a moment and think about why you started this race in the first place. You may have to revisit the goal and the party statement you wrote down. When you remember why you're doing what you do, you get where you wish to go with much more enthusiasm and success. You may come to realize that your desire to continue with the goal has changed because perhaps your values have changed. I have a friend who spent her entire life preparing to be a full time lawyer until the birth of her child. She then decided to be a full time mom. What changed? She still had a love for wanting to be a lawyer but she valued her new born child more. As a result, she redirected her goals altogether.

What is important here is not to get down on yourself or be discouraged if you are feeling unsure about your efforts and goals. Feeling frustrated is okay. Let me explain. Frustration is not necessarily a bad thing. Frustration simply says you know it should be working but it is not yet. I get frustrated when I can't get my baby's car seat in the car right or when I can't program my VCR. I know it's possible, I just have not yet figured it out! With frustration there is still hope inside of you. What is important now, whether you are feeling frustrated or discouraged, is to remember this can be another hidden opportunity. You just have to learn how to make it work for you. What an awesome opportunity to take time out to reflect on your original direction and to revisit your values. To look back over your journey and see where you got off track and what needs to be done to get back on track. The key is to keep the right attitude towards these distractions and see them as opportunities to learn and grow, then point yourself back in the direction of your goals, with renewed commitment and enthusiasm. Thomas Edison said it best when he said that "many of life's biggest regrets are people who did not realize how close they were to success when they gave up." Remember that in every setback there is an opportunity to regroup, energize yourself and move further than before. Consider a bow and arrow. The further the bow is pulled back the faster and further the arrow will go. Likewise, the more you are pulled back, the more potential you can develop for moving forward. What we sometimes need is what I call the Almighty Second Wind.

Have you ever watched a boxing match and just when you think one guy has taken a bad beating and he is about to go down for the count, then all of a sudden he finds this burst of energy and fights on? You know what they call that, right? "Second wind." Every now and then that's what we need when pursuing our goals. That second wind. That new fresh energy, idea or person that gets us rejuvenated. Some people have a habit of only going so far before they call it quits. For many, it is time sensitive. After about three months of doing something they slow down or stop. For others, they are satisfied with the feeling of a good effort toward accomplishing their goal rather than accomplishing their goal. It is almost like there is an invisible line that won't be crossed.

I am reminded of the caged lion that spent the first ten years of its life caged in a 15 foot by 15 foot cage. He would spend its days walking back and forth in the cage. When the day came for the lion to be set free in the wild it still would only walk about 15 feet before it turned back around. With no physical boundaries holding it back. The mental boundaries the lion developed now stops it from roaming free and becoming the king it should be. It's necessary to push ourselves past our normal stopping place. Unless you try to do something beyond what you have already mastered, you will never grow.

Creative Thinking

One of the most effective ways to help make it through the tougher and/or slower moments of reaching your goal is found in the form of creative thinking. Creativity has the power to stir up new ideas, create short cuts, and even save you time and money. This seems so simple and obvious that we oftentimes look right past it as the answer to take us to the next level. The root of creativity is called imagination. Remember that everything ever done, or said, or created was first an object of somebody's imagination. Think about the things you have already accomplished in life. Sometime earlier you imagined yourself accomplishing those tasks. Whether it was graduating, getting a certain job or meeting somebody special. It all starts with your imagination. Your imagination can be a preview of what is to come. It is now time to tap once again into this valuable asset that you control. Always keep in mind that there is a way to get where you desire to go. Success is not a matter of "if." It is a matter of "how." You should not tell yourself, "If I could get better opportunities...." Instead, you should say, "How can I get better opportunities?"

Take the time to imagine a better situation. Allow your mind to flow with no boundaries into the wonderful world of new and amazing possibilities. Children are awesome at this. Simply because their minds have no limitations or constraints deriving from "too much" education. I once asked a group of adults and kids to draw a picture of an alien like we have never seen before and then explain how they exist. Wouldn't you know that the pictures the adults drew looked like every other alien you see in documentaries, books and television. You know the one with the white bodies, bald heads and huge black eyes. Whereas, 9 out of 10 of the kid's aliens had no eyes no feet or noses. None of the features that are required on humans were found on these aliens. There shapes were abstract and reasons for their existence were literally out of this world. Their explanations and illustrations were so uninhibited and creative they inspired the adults to want to try again.

It's this type of inspiring creativity you want to tap into. It's time to draw from all kinds of resources of creativity such as dreams, childhood memories, sense perceptions and intuition, and people. You don't have to be highly educated or have a lot of resources to be creative. Some of the most creative people I have ever seen are those who lack both. Try driving in some of the poorer neighborhoods and see what you see. Kids turning trash bags into "slip and slides," trash can lids into snow sleds, and making go-carts out of lawn mowers.

When Booker T. Washington was a child, he yearned for education. Being a slave, he was unable to pursue his dream of going to school simply because it was illegal to educate slaves. But being the creative thinker that Booker was, he found a way to educate himself. Booker used to carry the books for his slave master's daughters in Franklin County. Oftentimes he would sit under the window of the school trying to listen to what was being taught in class. Many times when school was over and he would carry his slave master's daughter's books home, he would challenge the daughter to teach him. He would say, "I bet you can't teach me what they taught you in school today." And of course the young lady would say, "Uh huh." So Booker would say, "Then teach me." And it was here, on these long walks home, that Booker T Washington was able to find a creative way to get what he wanted. An education.

The art of being creative really begins with the art of questioning. Questioning our assumptions, beliefs and the way it is normally done. Once again, consider why children are so creative. They continually ask questions that are born out of a desire to understand and out of curiosity. Questioning expands our capacity to see more clearly and inspires us to explore possibilities we would otherwise ignore.

Get your creative juices flowing by first asking the right questions. Start by asking questions like: How can I make this better? What needs to be changed? What would be perfect or what is not working for me right now? Then move to more brainstorming questions like "What if." You will be amazed at the type of new avenues you can find when asking the right questions. All it takes is a willingness to think beyond the limits of your normal assumptions.

Final Thoughts

Your second wind can be found somewhere along the road to success. In order to find it, you must keep moving forward. The only way you will not be successful is if you decide to quit. Even if you find yourself in the middle of a storm, just keep moving. Remember, you don't have to wait for a storm to pass to get through it. Just keep moving forward and you will pass the storm. You owe it to yourself to go all the way. You deserve the end result. Think about it—your choices are simple. You can decide to give up now, and by doing so you can settle for less than what you deserve, or you can continue on this journey of success for as long as it takes to achieve what you've set out to achieve. Regardless of what you decided know that time will pass, no matter what you do. You don't want to look back at this day as one where you gave up but rather as a day where you got up! Time will keep on going. Your best strategy is to keep on going, too. Be creative, nurture the right relationships and neuter the bad ones. Take advantage of every minute that you have. If you find yourself without enough energy, then find a resting place. Take time to enjoy that benchmark while you rest. Then get back up and keep on going. Remember your destiny is tapping its foot waiting on you to make things happen. You are here to make a difference. Keep on moving forward, find that almighty second wind and by doing so you will create a level of confidence, thrill and achievement that you otherwise could have never known.

CHAPTER 11

Eliminating the Stress of Success: Balance

It was one of my favorite scenes in one of my favorite movies, *The Karate Kid*. Mr. Miyagi was teaching Daniel the fine art of karate. In doing so, he took him out on a row boat and had him stand with his feet planted on the sides of the boat. This didn't sit well with Daniel, who just wanted to learn to fight. However, Mr. Miyagi wanted him to first learn balance. As Daniel kept insisting to learn fighting maneuvers, Mr. Miyagi rocked the boat roughly, knocking Daniel into the water. With that, Mr. Miyagi tells him again, "First, you must learn balance!"

Well, if you expect to stay on your feet for long, you must also learn balance. If you're like most people, you have many things going on at once. You're trying to juggle work, a marriage, children, personal time, sleep, an exercise regimen, you name it. And without balance, it's just a matter of time before one of these various balls gets "dropped." Important tasks at work are left undone, causing damage to your career and costing your employer money. Or worse, your relationship with your family gets neglected, causing an even worse form of pain. Whenever any ball gets "dropped," you experience feelings of guilt, failure, shame and emptiness. Obviously, these are the feelings that most of us want to avoid at all costs. Therefore, learning balance is absolutely crucial. What good is success if it's accompanied by feelings of guilt, failure, shame and emptiness?

I meet many successful people in my travels. It's one of the biggest perks of being a professional speaker. I'm constantly learning lessons from these remarkable men and women. And one of the biggest lessons I've learned is the importance of balance. Time and time again, I've met people who have achieved "success" on a level that few people could even imagine. Yet, they would be the first to admit that the price they paid for their success was too high. They traded in spouses, children, family members and even a relationship with God in pursuit of a dream. And while in the end they "won," what they lost was far more valuable.

In fact, Billy Joel stressed this point in an interview. As you know, Billy Joel is one of the most successful singer/songwriters in the last two decades. During the 1980s alone, Joel recorded an astounding *twenty* Top 40 hits, nine of which reached the Top 10. He has received awards for Male Artist of the Year, Record of the Year, Song of the Year, and Album of the Year. He was also inducted into the Rock and Roll Hall of Fame. In short, you couldn't ask for more success than this as a musician. How could you ask for anything more, right? Well, here is what he had to say in an interview shortly after being inducted into the Hall of Fame:

"The happiest times in my life were when my relationships were going well. But in my whole life, I haven't met the person I can sustain a relationship with yet. So I'm discontented about that. I'm angry with myself. I have regrets. You don't get hugged by the Rock and Roll Hall of Fame, and you don't have children with the Rock and Roll Hall of Fame. I want what everybody else wants: to love and to be loved, and to have a family."

This is a point I continually stress with myself. As a push towards reaching my professional dreams, I have to remind myself about what's really important—my wife and two daughters. Speaking is how I make my living but my family is what makes my life worth living. One of the saddest things that I can imagine is to make it to the top of my profession *by myself.*

When you're pursuing your calling in life, it's tempting to become obsessed with it. Your every waking thought becomes consumed with, "How do I get there and how can I make it happen now?" As a result, even when you are at home, you're not really there. Sure, your physical body is there but your mind is miles away at the next sales presentation, production meeting or wherever. This isn't helpful to anyone.

Therefore, one key to maintaining balance is to be where you are. In other words, wherever you are, you should be there body and soul. If you're at work, your time and attention should be exclusively focused on business. Likewise, when you're at home, your time and attention should be focused on your family. You must make yourself available to your family, both physically and mentally.

Remember, your family members don't care how much you know, they only want to know how much you care. After all, my two daughters Mia and Sydnee couldn't care less if I have the ability to speak to thousands. Nor do they care if I have the ability to motivate others. There is only one ability that they care about – my *availability*. Therefore, I must be available to them; available to play with them, available to talk to them about school, available to help them learn to read and write, and available just to sit them on my knee and let them know that their Daddy loves them. However, I can't do any of these things if I become consumed with the next speech or getting the next corporate training contract.

However, that's what far too many people do. They attempt to "multitask" in the name of efficiency. They figure that while they're at home for the weekend, they'll write a few quick memos, read the latest market forecast and prepare a few projections. However, in most cases, this person ends up doing very little of anything productive. Not only do they not spend quality time with their families but they don't get much work done either.

For this reason you must learn to effectively use the most important resource available to you—time. It's more valuable than silver and gold and seemingly, just as scarce. It's the one thing that most people wish they had more of. Some people have enough money. Some people have enough friends or enough social activities. But no one ever seems to have enough time. Time is the currency of life.

Think about it. Most of us are paid for our time. We don't live off our investments. Most of us don't even sell a product. We make our living by selling our time to others. It's the one true source of wealth that everyone possesses. For this reason, we must carefully guard our time.

This is particularly true because time is limited. Each of us has just 24 hours of time to "spend" each day. Regardless of whether you are Donald Trump or the greeter at Wal-Mart, you only have 24 hours to use each day. The quantity of time is the same for each of us. However, what makes the difference in life is the *quality* of time. Or, in other words, how you use your time will determine the quality of your life. If you use your time wisely, you can live a dynamic and fulfilled life. On the other hand, if you aimlessly squander your time, your life will be filled with a series of "wouldas," and "shouldas."

We have discussed in detail the hazards of not giving enough time and effort to our family. And we certainly know the dangers of being a workaholic or becoming obsessed with your dreams.

However, I want to take a moment to warn you about the dangers of not giving enough time and effort to your hobbies and personal interests. For many people, whenever they become pressed for time, the first choice is to forego these activities. They neglect their reading time or they give up their weekly basketball game at the gym. The thought is that these activities are frivolous so they can be done without.

Nonetheless, you shouldn't reach this conclusion too quickly. Oftentimes, your hobbies have ancillary benefits. For example, if you spend your reading time learning about the latest techniques in your field or just becoming inspired by the stories of others, then your reading time is important. The same could be true of giving up a hobby like playing basketball or racquetball. These hobbies provide you with a much-needed physical boost as well as allow you to form relationships with others. Your hobbies are often very valuable to your overall success.

Besides, it's important to realize that sometimes, the most productive thing you can do is to take a break. This is often referred to as "sharpening the saw." This reference is to the practice employed by lumberjacks. Lumberjacks have discovered that they can cut more trees in less time by taking period breaks to sharpen their saws. You and I must do the same thing.

Sometimes, we must simply sit down and relax. For some people, this would involve running a long, hot bath and just soaking in the tub for an hour or so. For others, sharpening the saw means taking a walk or a drive in the country. And for others, sharpening the saw may be a vacation to Tahiti or a weekend at a spa resort. Of course, no one way is better than another. The important thing is that you sharpen that saw.

In the final analysis, if you are like most of us, then you don't just want success; you want *good* success. Believe it or not, there is such a thing as bad success. Bad success is when you've finally built a lucrative business but you have ulcers, and your daughter feels that you don't love her and your wife has begun to have an affair because she's lonely. That's bad success and it happens when you get out of balance.

On the other hand, good success is a successful business *and* good health, happy children and a loving marriage. Good success is having it all and that's only possible if you keep your life in balance. In the words of my aunt, the key is to "work a little, play a little, love a little, rest a little, give a little and pray a lot." By doing so, you will find happiness and balance in your life.

Perhaps for this reason, there are a number of time management techniques out there. And many of them are valid and workable. However, not all techniques are introduced independent of any real direction. As a result, they teach you how to better accomplish tasks that take you no closer to your real goals. This is like getting a shortcut to the wrong destination. It's better than taking the long way there, but not entirely helpful.

For this reason, I think that it's important to integrate time management techniques that will help you accomplish your goals and values. To do so, let's complete the following exercise. In the box on the next page, on the left, list the people and things that are most important to you. The people will most likely be family members, close friends and perhaps co-workers, etc. The things could be anything. Examples may include organizations, physical traits such as being physically fit, financial security, whatever the case may be. The most important thing here is not to leave anything out. Next in the box below, on the right, list the activities you spend most of your time and energy doing.

Things and People I Value Most	Activities That Take Up My Time & Energy

Take time now to compare your boxes. Are the things that you have identified as most important to you the same things you spend your time and energy doing? If not, it may be time to shed some of things that take up your time but are not really that important to you. By doing so, you may find yourself able to balance that which is important to you. A person's value system has a way of shaping their goals in life. For example if you value good health, you will make time for daily exercise and proper nutrition. If you value career satisfaction, you will take time to improve your work performance. What is important to note here is that your values will not prevent you from reaching your ultimate destination, but they will affect the route that you take. Oftentimes, when you are faced with competing priorities, or you have too much to do in too little time, you cannot do everything. Every decision you make regarding how you will spend your time impacts all the potential ways you could be spending that time. Therefore, it is important to clarify and prioritize each of your goals with respect to all of your other commitments.

Sometimes, it is a matter of saying no to some things so you can say yes to others. I have learned that it is a lot easier saying "no" to something when you know there is a greater "yes" somewhere else. And it is easier to say good-bye to some people when there is a greater hello somewhere else. I can remember watching *48 Hours* on television when they were interviewing a man who had given up drinking alcohol after struggling with drinking for over twenty years. When asked how he was able to say no to drinking after abusing it for so long he said it was easy. He simply decided to say yes to keeping his family. By remembering what is most important and what you value is often the best way to shed what is not.

Another exercise that can be done to help you keep balance in your life is to take a look at how well you're balancing your priorities. We can do this by dividing your day into four parts: Work/ Job, Relationships/ Family, Hobbies/Interest, Personal time (feel free to choose your own priorities). In this exercise, list how many hours a day or week you spend with each. For example I spend 6 hours at work but then I spend an hour at home thinking or doing more work. So all together I spend 7 hours a day doing work stuff. Likewise, I spend 30 minutes eating breakfast with my family. I also spend evenings from 5 until 10 o'clock with my wife and kids, so I can say I spend 5.5 hours a day with my family.

If by chance, most of your days carry different schedules (which for most people it does) you may want to calculate how many hours in a week rather than a day. By doing this exercise, you should have a clearer vision of how much time is being spent in these areas. The pie chart below is designed to help you see how you divide your time.

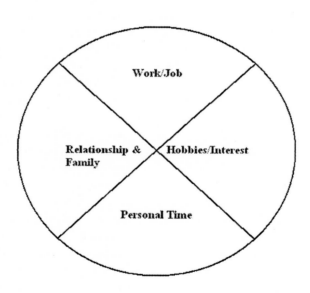

Final Thoughts

Getting carried away in your goal is easy to do when you're excited about it. Your goals automatically become an integral part of your life, and often, the line between your goal and life itself gets so blurred that the difference becomes intangible. It's for this reason it is important to know that most successful people credit a balanced life as their key to success.

To master true balance, a person needs to first know how to maintain equilibrium between rest and activity. Going, going, going, and doing, doing, doing, will only leave you tired, tired, tired. It is important to be able to maintain equilibrium between activity and rest. One reason for this is that one greatly influences the other. If you work hard you should rest well. And if you rest well you should be able to work hard. Too much of either will result in deficiency of the other. It is important to be committed to following through with your goal in life, yet you should spend some time apart from it as well. On a regular basis, you should take a break and keep balance in your life by giving attention to other things that are important in your life as well. This will give you a chance to re-energize yourself and re-focus your mind upon the things, which are truly important to you. One of these things being our relationships with loved ones.

Having a balanced life does not mean that each day of your life must be balanced or perfectly divided. Each day will look different. For instance, some work days require excessively long hours, certain goals takes days of preparation, and some people deserve time when they ask. Seasons can also dictate what type of balance you have going on in life. During the holidays, you might find yourself spending less time working and more time with family. Sometimes balance is divided into days of the week. Many people get more sleep and relaxation on the weekends so they have the needed physical and mental energy to forge ahead during the workweek. Many spiritual people have a holy day each week, which they devote primarily to worship. Living a balanced life is seeing life as a big picture and not just a series of days. What's most important is that you give enough time for all the important things and people in your life.

CHAPTER 12

"Pay It Forward"

One day I found myself staring at a drunken man on the side of the road. I could not help but wonder if things were different could this have been the person to find the cure for cancer. Or perhaps the next great civil rights leader. As I sat there and watched this man, I had come to my own conclusion that this was not what he had planned for his life. That surely, he had dreams and aspirations higher than his present reality. And although I never point fingers or judge others, I couldn't help but wonder, how many others have let there dreams die because they never took a chance on the best opportunity they had… themselves. Unfortunately, some people will leave this life with regrets of not doing what was in their heart to do. Sadly, there is no cure for regret. The best thing we can do now is take advantage of the opportunity we have now to follow our passions.

When you follow your true passion in life, you bring something to this world nobody else can give. You bring an energy, delight and service that radiates from the joy you find in living your dream. It is as if you were created to do just that—live out your dreams. And if you decided not to follow your passion, something would be missing in the world that no one else can replace. After all, nobody can write your book but you, nobody can start up a business like yours. Nor can anybody cook or season food like you do. You are as unique as your fingerprint and nobody can take your place. Others may try, but nobody can do what you do quite like you.

When you follow your passion, you have the opportunity to change the world. It is amazing what an impact you can have on others when you follow your dream. I have been forever changed simply because of other people living out their dreams.

Years ago there was a doctor named Dr. Cherry who followed his heart to become a children's surgeon, and a young lady by the name of Rene who decided to follow her passion to be a speech therapist. As a result of these two people following their dreams, I can now stand tall, speak clearly and follow my dreams. From here, it is now my pleasure and opportunity to take my dream and use it to motivate others to live theirs. In doing so I am participating in what Catherine Ryan calls "Paying it forward"

Catherine Ryan is a well-known author who has written many novels such as *Funerals for Horses* and *Earthquake Weather*. However, she is probably best known for the book turned to movie called *Pay It Forward*. The idea behind this title is if someone did you a favor—something big, something you could not do for yourself—instead of trying to pay it back, you paid it forward by doing something for someone else. The concept behind this is that we could trigger a change reaction that could change people's life for the better.

A few years back I was asked to come speak to an organization called Stay Clean, a rehabilitation center for men and women who have been addicted to drugs and alcohol. I came to motivate them and give them encouragement. I can remember speaking to them for at least forty-five minutes on the power they have inside of them and how to tap into that power to overcome addictions.

Once I had completed my motivational talk, many participants came to speak to me. I shook hands and gave more encouraging words to everyone I could. I could tell there was one man who sitting to the side waiting for me to finish so he could speak to me one on one. As I turned towards him, I saw why he was sitting. He was bound to a wheelchair. He rolled my direction with what seemed to be watery eyes. He then proceeded to tell me things about myself that I had not shared with the group. He knew the schools I went to, who my family was, he even new about my legs and stuttering problems. I asked him if we had met before. He then looked me in the eyes and said, "You don't remember me do you?" I apologized and told him I did not. He said, "My name is Dolan."

The same guy who gave me such a hard time growing up as a child in Portland, Oregon. The one who picked me first for kick-ball so the other kids could laugh at the way I kicked the ball and ran. He was the one I used to hide from when walking down the halls of Sellwood Middle School, afraid he would make fun of the speech classes I had to go to.

Now, here he was, sitting in front of me in a wheelchair, looking up to me for words of encouragement. I asked him what had happened to him since I had seen him last. He told me twenty years ago after I had moved out of state, he began using drugs. And one day, he got behind the wheel of a car and was driving the wrong way on a one-way street and was struck and is now paralyzed from the waist down.

I have to be honest here and tell you when he first told this my first instinct was to take advantage of the situation. After he took advantage of me years ago. Now I had him right where I wanted him! But when I opened my mouth, all that came out were the kindest and most encouraging words I knew. This was my opportunity to show him what I wanted him to know years ago. It does not matter what you look like on the outside but what you are made of in the inside. This was my perfect opportunity to "Pay it forward." After all, Dolan had a lot to do with my desire to make something out of myself. All the name calling, teasing, and knocking me down he did gave me motivation to build confidence and better myself. I took that fear of him and turned it into fuel to put me where I wanted to be—successful.

There was no need for me to seek revenge from Dolan. Success is the greatest revenge there is. But more important than that, from that day forward, Dolan became my biggest fan. I have received more speaking engagements as a result of Dolan spreading the word about my presentations than I have through any other source. All because I decided to "pay it forward."

You, too, can "pay it forward" with whatever goal you wish to reach. Even if you think your goal is more of a personal accomplishment and not one to impact the world. For example, we have all heard of the remarkable stories of those who have lost massive amounts of weight to live more healthy and happy lives. And although the fact they lost weight does not affect us directly, it does inspire us and motivate us to better ourselves. And the same will be true with you. Once you reach your goals and start living your dreams, people around you will be encouraged to do the same. And you to will be caught up in the great movement of "paying it forward."

CHAPTER 13

All That It Takes Is All That You've Got

I used to wonder what would cause someone to spend a lifetime reaching their goals and why others try for 15 minutes and then give up. Why some people will work as hard as they can and others try to find the easiest way of doing things. Or what causes someone to invest most of their life in one career and then out of the blue, switch to something new? I have realized that for the most part, people are in search of success and happiness. However, success is whatever you have determined success to be. For some it is fame, for some fortune, and for others it is feeling secure and happy with themselves. However you define success, remember you have what it takes to reach it. You've got what it takes to succeed and you have what it takes to triumph over the little distractions, and the big problems. Nonetheless, what some fail to realize is that many times it will take everything you have to reach that point. But isn't it worth it?

In this book, I have shared with you the best insights I've learned about success and happiness. I sincerely hope that you've found some keys in this book that will help you to unlock your destiny. In fact, if you've found just one useful tip or hint in this book, I truly believe that this exercise has been useful for both of us.

Very often, we read a good book and make the mistake of saying something like, "Wow! That's good stuff! One of these days, I'm going to try that!" I have to admit that I've been guilty of doing this on a few occasions myself. However, let's face it. Nothing written in this book will do you a world of good unless you apply it to your own life. And the time to do so is *now*.

Too often in life, we live under the illusion of "someday." We think of a magical someday when all of our bills are paid, our kids are raised, our health is perfect and the economy is booming and we say, "That's the day that I'm going to start using some of the things I've learned about success over the years." There will always be some circumstance in your life that could be better. Sometimes, you just have to start where you are now and take the future as it comes. Kobi Yamada would say, "Sometimes you have to take the leap, and build your wings on the way down."

Besides, "someday" isn't promised to any of us. There are no guarantees about what the next decade will hold. In fact, there aren't any guarantees about what the next year, month or even week will hold for any of us. We simply never know how much time we have left on this planet to make the difference that, I believe, we were put here to make. Therefore, it's important that we forget about those "somedays" and start looking towards TO-DAY.

What can you do *today* to start working towards a better future? Do you need to build your energy? Perhaps, you could enroll at a health club or resolve to quit smoking today. Or maybe you need to start looking the part. If so, perhaps you could go out and buy a new business suit or have an existing suit taken in (or out) a little bit to make it fit better. Of course, the possibilities here are endless. The important thing is that you take action to turn your dreams into a reality and there's no better time to start than now. Resolve to do just one thing *today*. It could be the start of a whole new you and that's really what this is all about… you.

Today is the day you should start fulfilling your best possibilities. Today is the day to make things happen. Remember problems don't go away by themselves but opportunities do. Somehow problems just get bigger unattended and opportunity goes to knock on someone else's door. So do not procrastinate about anything. If there is a problem that is holding you back from moving forward, change your attitude about the problem and turn your problem into a possibility for success. If opportunity is knocking, answer the door. Now is the time you have available to you and today is when your goals, your dreams, your ambitions begin to become a reality. Mark this day on your calendar, because after today you will never be the same. Consider today as the day you rise up from just talking about your dreams and begin to live your dreams.

Every moment is yours—with which to work, to build, to create, and to live with passion and purpose. Life is great and you're a wonderful, dynamic, creative person. You have what it takes to set yourself free from whatever limitations there may be and move confidently towards your destination. Likewise you have what it takes to look into the face of opposition and melt it into your opportunity. Remember, all that it takes is all that you've got and all that you've got is all it takes.

Finally I close this book with one of the most inspiring stories during the Sydney 2000 Summer Olympics.

Eric Moussambani is a 22-year-old student from a country in western Africa, Equatorial Guinea. With a national population of 400,000, Equatorial Guinea formed its swimming federation less than a year ago and was able to send Eric to the Olympics under a special program that permits poorer countries to participate even though their athletes don't meet the customary standards.

Unfortunately, the federation had only two pools that Eric could use for training. Both of these pools were located within hotels and were very short in length. Eric was only allowed to train for one hour at a time, three times a week. Unlike other Olympians who had been training for years, Eric could not begin his training until eight months before the Olympics.

On Tuesday, September 19, Eric was to swim in his qualifying heat for the 100-meter freestyle. The starter's gun sounded, and the two other swimmers in his heat were disqualified for hitting the water too quickly. Now Eric would have to swim alone in a one-man race against himself.

He never put his head under the water's surface. With ten meters left to the wall, he virtually came to a stop. Some spectators thought he actually might drown. Nevertheless he pressed forward and gave it all he had. His time was the slowest in Olympic history, a dismal 1:52.72.

Nevertheless he did it! He did what he set him mind and heart to do. He went to the Olympic games and he competed with the world's best. Though he didn't class with the other swimmers involved, he won the hearts of millions simply by finishing the race.

"I never swam the 100 meters before," Eric said. "All the clapping and all those voices making noise helped me finish."

It is my desire that this book provides the clapping and noise you need to help you finish your race to your goals! So when it is all said and done you to can say "I did it!" Remember all that it takes is all that you've got and all that you've got is all it takes!

S Holy Book -
O Genesis: Pg 36 - re. past

N Fall/Egypt:

D Exodus:
   J 10 Commandments:
Promised Land/Revelation:

Mission/gifts: pg 110, pg 30

Disciples: pg 19

Golgotha:

Sanctification:

Printed in the United States
30290LVS00001B/436-534

9 781413 771749